D1214605

VOLUME **7**

AUXILIARY ELECTRICAL EQUIPMENT

Author R. G. Brunner

Written by
Stone & Webster Engineering Corporation
245 Summer Street
Boston, Massachusetts 02107

Electric Power Research Institute
3412 Hillview Avenue
Palo Alto, California 94304

EPRI Project Manager
D. K. Sharma

Ordering Information

Requests for copies of this series should be directed
to Research Reports Center (RRC), P.O. Box 50490,
Palo Alto, CA 94303, (415) 965-4081.

For further information on EPRI's technical pro-
grams contact the EPRI Technical Information Division at (415) 855-2411, or write directly to EPRI's
Technical Information Center at P.O. Box 10412, Palo
Alto, CA 94303.

EL-5036, Volume 7
Project 2334

ISBN 0-8033-5006-6 volume
ISBN 0-8033-5015-5 series

Topics: Electric arcs
        Circuit breakers
        Switchgear
        Auxiliary switching equipment
        Maintenance

Copyright © 1987 Electric Power Research Institute, Inc.
All rights reserved.

Electric Power Research Institute and EPRI are registered
service marks of Electric Power Research Institute, Inc.

Notice

This series was prepared by Stone & Webster Engineering
Corporation as an account of work sponsored by the Electric Power Research Institute, Inc. (EPRI). Neither EPRI,
members of EPRI, Stone & Webster Engineering Corporation, nor any person acting on behalf of any of them:
(a) makes any warranty, express or implied, with respect to
the use of any information, apparatus, method, or process
disclosed in this series or that such use may not infringe
privately owned rights, or (b) assumes any liabilities with
respect to the use of, or for damages resulting from the
use of, any information, apparatus, method, or process disclosed in this series.

FOREWORD

In the past, several electrical equipment manufacturers published reference books dealing with specific technical areas. Many utilities have stated that these reference books have been very useful to them in dealing with plant emergencies and in making decisions on design, system planning, and preventive maintenance.

Unfortunately, manufacturers today seldom publish or update reference books on electric power apparatus, mainly because of tighter budget constraints. Until now, utilities have had no up-to-date industrywide practical reference manual covering the various electric power apparatus and electrical phenomena commonly encountered in power plants. The Power Plant Electrical Reference Series was planned to fill this need.

EPRI believes that the series will save utilities time and money. It will aid plant engineers in

- Prevention of forced outages through proper installation, application, and protection of station auxiliary equipment

- Recognition of potential problems and their prevention

- Selection of appropriate methods of maintenance to ensure trouble-free equipment operation

- Reduction of equipment installation time and expense

- Proper specification of equipment being ordered

- Better coordination and integration of system components

This volume deals with power plant auxiliary electrical equipment. Load-switching and fault-interrupting equipment is an important part of the power plant station service auxiliary system. It provides a means for controlled switching of electrical equipment and provides coordinated short-circuit and overload protection for station service equipment. The application of station service switching equipment, which consists of switchgear, secondary unit substations, motor control centers, and generator circuit breakers, must be well defined before this equipment can be correctly specified.

Information about the application of station service electrical equipment is available in the publications and standards of technical societies, in engineering handbooks, and in manufacturers' literature. This volume additionally provides the overall performance requirements of the station service auxiliary equipment. It guides the user in applying the industry standards for power plants.

The goal of this volume is to describe the technological advances in load-switching and fault-interrupting equipment. A selection and a review of applicable published literature and industry standards were performed to guide generating-station personnel in the design, procurement, testing, and maintenance of this equipment. This volume discusses the available types of equipment and delineates the system requirements and the diagnostics for problems unique to this type of equipment.

D. K. Sharma

Plant Electrical Systems and Equipment Program
Electrical Systems Division
Electric Power Research Institute

ABSTRACT

Load-switching and fault-interrupting equipment is an essential component of the power plant auxiliary system. It provides a means of switching electrical loads and provides controlled, coordinated short-circuit and overload protection for all station service equipment.

This volume describes the types of auxiliary electrical equipment and delineates their advantages, disadvantages, and applications, along with suggested maintenance and diagnostics for problems unique to each type of equipment. Diagrams explain the operation of:

- Medium-voltage switchgear: oil, air-magnetic, vacuum, sulfur hexafluoride, and air-blast circuit breakers

- Secondary unit substations: disconnect switches, air-magnetic circuit breakers, and transformers (liquid-insulated, dry-type, and cast-coil)

- Motor control centers

- Panel boards

- Generator breakers

- Bus: isolated-phase, segregated-phase, and nonsegregated-phase

In addition, the volume contains examples that explain how to select circuit breakers and how to replace an old circuit breaker with a modern one. Environmental considerations, such as abnormal temperatures, high altitudes, and exposure to moisture, metal dust, vibration, and other hostile environments, are also included.

ACKNOWLEDGMENTS

The author wishes to express his appreciation to the following people for their guidance, reviews, and comments.

Electric Power Research Institute

D. K. Sharma, Project Manager
R. Steiner, Associate Director, Electrical Systems Division
G. Addis, Project Manager
L. Kolarik, Technical Assistant to Division Director
J. C. White, Program Manager

Stone & Webster Engineering Corporation

G. O. Buffington, Project Manager
E. P. Donegan
A. R. Fitzpatrick
P. Garfinkel
A. P. Stakutis

EPRI Review Committee

J. R. Boyle, Tennessee Valley Authority
L. E. Brothers, Southern Company Services
J. Erlingsson, Pacific Gas and Electric Company
R. G. Farmer, Arizona Public Service Company
R. G. Hodgson, Los Angeles Department of Water & Power
J. A. Maxwell, Georgia Power Company
W. L. Nail, Jr., Mississippi Power & Light Company
D. G. Owen, Duke Power Company
B. K. Patel, Southern Company Services
R. A. Schaefer, Public Service Company of Oklahoma
J. E. Stoner, Jr., Duke Power Company
D. M. Van Tassell, Jr., Florida Power & Light Company
J. E. White, Tampa Electric Company

The author also extends thanks to G. N. Lester of Boston Edison Company for his valuable suggestions and for his careful review of the final manuscript.

CONTENTS

FIGURES

TABLES

EXECUTIVE SUMMARY

Power-switching and system protection equipment provides the means for distributing the station auxiliary power supply to plant equipment drives. The application and maintenance of this equipment and an understanding of the applicable industry standards are vital to the continued operation of the power plant.

Background

The industry standards governing the manufacture of circuit breakers and associated plant auxiliary equipment have changed considerably since the 1960s, and the effects of these changes have not been fully appreciated by engineers. Older equipment has to be replaced with equipment manufactured to different standards; it is essential to understand the meaning of equipment ratings in order to correctly apply the equipment.

Objective

This volume aims to develop guidelines for the design, procurement, installation, testing, and maintenance of the station service auxiliary power supply equipment. It also means to identify modern practices and requirements for medium-voltage switchgear, secondary unit substations, motor control equipment, and generator circuit breakers.

Approach

Pertinent information was accumulated from a national survey of utility requirements. A search of literature about station service auxiliary equipment was performed to identify specific information on power plant applications. Additionally, the EPRI Review Committee, with members from 11 utilities in various areas of the United States, and other industry experts reviewed the material for technical adequacy and completeness. This information provided the basis for this volume of the Power Plant Electrical Reference Series.

Results

The material in this volume is expected to provide guidance for the engineering and operating departments of generating facilities in selecting satisfactory equipment and replacement components for a reliable station service auxiliary system.

ACRONYMS
&
ABBREVIATIONS

A	ampere(s)
ac	alternating current
AIEE	American Institute of Electrical Engineers (now Institute of Electrical and Electronics Engineers [IEEE])
ANSI	American National Standards Institute
ASTM	American Society for Testing and Materials
BIL	basic impulse insulation level
C_E	energy cost in dollars per kilowatt (Eq. 7-7)
C_I	installed transformer cost (Eq. 7-9)
cm	centimeter(s)
C_o	total annual operating cost (Eq. 7-7)
CF_4	carbon tetrafluoride
$C_2Cl_3F_3$	trichlorotrifluoroethane
$Cl_2{:}CCl_2$	perchloroethylene
CH_3SCH_3	dimethyl sulfide
CH_3SH	methyl mercaptan
CO	close-open
CPT	control power transformer
C_{pv}	present value of total annual operating cost (Eq. 7-8)
CS_2	carbon disulfide
C_T	total transformer cost
D	day(s) per year transformer operates (Eq. 7-7)
dc	direct current
E	millivolt drop across contacts (Eq. 7-10)
F	fraction of 100% load expected on the transformer (Eq. 7-6)
F_3CCF_3	hexafluoroethane
F_2SO	thionyl fluoride
H	hour(s) per day transformer operates (Eq. 7-7)
HCl	hydrogen chloride
HF	hydrogen fluoride
hp	horsepower
H_2S	hydrogen sulfide
HV	high voltage
Hz	hertz
i	rate of return
I	current
ICS	Industrial Controls and Systems
IEEE	Institute of Electrical and Electronics Engineers, Inc.
in.	inch(es)

K	rated voltage range factor K
kA	kiloampere(s)
kAIC	kiloamperes interrupting current
KEMA	Laboratory and Research Center, Arnheim, Netherlands
kHz	kilohertz
kV	kilovolt(s)
kVA	kilovolt(s) amperes
L_{EL}	total transformer losses at expected load (Eq. 7-6)
L_c	core losses (Eq. 7-6)
L_T	total winding losses at full load (Eq. 7-6)
LV	low voltage
MCC	motor control center
MCP	motor circuit protection
MOC	mechanism-operated control
ms	millisecond(s)
μs	microsecond(s)
MV	medium voltage
MVA	megavolt ampere(s)
N	years of postulated transformer life
N_2	nitrogen
NEMA	National Electrical Manufacturers Association
O	open
OCS	carbonyl sulfide
ppm	parts per million
R	contact resistance (Eq. 7-10)
rms	root mean square
RTD	resistance temperature detector
s	second(s)
SO_2	sulfur dioxide
SF_6	sulfur hexafluoride
SUS	secondary unit substation
T	permissible tripping delay (Eq. 7-4)
TOC	truck-operated contact
V	volt(s)
Vac	volt(s) alternating current
Y	rated permissible tripping delay

AUXILIARY ELECTRICAL EQUIPMENT

R. G. Brunner

7.1 INTRODUCTION

Load-switching and fault-interrupting equipment is an important part of the power plant auxiliary service system. It provides a means for switching electrical equipment, in addition to providing controlled, coordinated short-circuit and overload protection for all station service equipment. It performs reliably and contributes in large measure to the dependability of modern electric power systems. This volume covers the application of switchgears, secondary-unit substations, motor control centers, generator circuit breakers, and buses.

The highest-capacity switching equipment in the power plant auxiliary service system is medium-voltage switchgear (2.4 to 38 kV), which provides distribution from the unit auxiliary transformer to various loads, such as large motors and secondary unit substations. Medium-voltage switchgear should be located in a clean, controlled environment, preferably near the transformers feeding them. Secondary unit substations have a transformer and low-voltage switchgear (208 to 600 V) and provide distribution to low-voltage loads, such as 100- to 500-hp motors, panel boards, and distribution transformers. Motor control centers, in turn, distribute low-voltage power to motors, commonly 100 hp or less, and some selected nonmotor loads when convenient. Secondary unit substations and motor control centers are located centrally to the loads served to minimize lead length and accompanying voltage drop. Secondary unit substations and motor control centers should also be in a clean, dry environment. If the environment is not clean and dry (and away from fluid-carrying piping systems), a suitable enclosure should be provided to exclude the contaminants. Panel boards are used to distribute power to all low-voltage nonmotor loads, such as lighting, heating, and convenience outlets. Panel boards are distributed throughout the plant close to the loads served.

The generator circuit breaker and isolated-phase bus connect the generator to the station unit transformer. A generator circuit breaker is not a mandatory component in a power generating station but has found application in some stations. For example, nuclear power stations are required to have two independent off-site power sources to ensure capability of safe shutdown and public safety, which may be met by using two startup transformers fed by two independent lines. One station service (startup) transformer and independent line may be eliminated by using a generator circuit breaker and feeding the internal plant requirements back through the unit transformer. With the generator circuit breaker open, the main transmission line is available as an off-site source.

The distinction between load-interrupting and fault-interrupting equipment is often misunderstood, which results in misapplications. Load-interrupting equipment, such as contactors and starters, are designed for perhaps 200,000 full-load operations with little or no maintenance but are not designed to interrupt fault currents. Circuit breakers are designed expressly for quick, efficient fault current interruption. Although circuit breakers will also switch load currents, they should not normally be used for large numbers of repetitive load operations. Indeed, applying a circuit breaker for highly repetitive duty may result in a worn-out breaker in a few years, or at least it may require extensive maintenance. If applied for repetitive load switching, a circuit breaker should be tested and rated by the manufacturer for such duty.

Throughout the life of a power generating plant, scheduled preventive maintenance must be performed to ensure that auxiliary service system equipment meets its original performance requirements. A maintenance plan will reduce equipment failures and identify aging equipment and components for expeditious replacement. Clearly, a planned maintenance program is a vital part of power generation reliability.

7.2 DEFINITION OF TERMS

Circuit breaker A mechanical switching device, capable of making, carrying, and breaking currents under normal conditions and also making, carrying for a specific time, and breaking currents under specified abnormal circuit conditions, such as those of short circuit.

Contactor A device for repeatedly establishing and interrupting an electric power circuit.

Disconnecting or isolating switch A mechanical switching device used for changing the connections in a circuit or for isolating a circuit or equipment from the source of power. It is required to carry normal load current continuously and abnormal or short-circuit currents for short intervals as specified. It is also required to open or close circuits either when negligible current is broken or made or when no significant change occurs in the voltage across the terminals of each of the switch poles.

Load-interrupter switch An interrupter switch designed to interrupt currents not in excess of the continuous-current rating of the switch. It may be designed to close and carry abnormal or short-circuit currents as specified.

Motor control center An assembly of motor controllers, having modular design to permit rearrangement, interchange, and easy replacement of modular parts.

Motor controller A device or group of devices that serves to govern, in some predetermined manner, the electric power delivered to the motor or group of motors to which it is connected.

Panel board A single panel or a group of panel units designed for assembly in the form of a single panel, including buses, with or without switches and/or automatic overcurrent protective devices for the control of light, heat, or power circuits. A panel board is designed to be placed in a cabinet or cutout box. It may be placed in a control board lineup, open or accessible from the rear.

Secondary-unit substation A unit substation in which the low-voltage section is rated 1000 V and below.

Station service (startup) transformer The transformer, connected to high-voltage transmission lines, used to feed station auxiliary loads during the station startup sequence.

Switchgear A general term covering switching and interrupting devices and their combination with associated control, instrumentation, metering, protective, and regulating devices.

Switchgear assembly Assembled equipment (indoor or outdoor) including, but not limited to, one or more of the following: switching, interrupting, control instrumentation, metering, protective and regulating, together with their supporting structures, enclosures, conductors, electric interconnections, and accessories.

Unit auxiliary transformer The transformer, connected to the generator bus, used to feed station auxiliary loads.

Unit substation A substation consisting primarily of one or more transformers that are mechanically and electrically connected to, and coordinated in design with, one or more switchgear or motor control assemblies or combinations thereof.

Unit transformer A power system supply transformer (generator step-up) that transforms all or a portion of the unit power from the unit (generator) to the power system voltage.

7.3 CIRCUIT BREAKERS—THEORY OF ARC INTERRUPTION

Although very different in appearance and interrupting medium (air, oil, vacuum, sulfur hexafluoride [SF_6]), all circuit breakers depend on the zero pause and deionization of the current path to effect current interruption.

ELECTRIC ARC CHARACTERISTICS—THE ZERO PAUSE

When the circuit breaker opens, the contacts separate and an electric arc flows between the separated contacts. A useful characteristic of an electric arc is that it requires a minimum burning voltage to be sustained. When the driving voltage goes below the minimum arc voltage, current flow substantially decreases; and the hot, ionized gases begin deionizing and dissipating. During the next fraction of a second, the dielectric strength of the gap between the separating contacts increases and, if the dielectric strength increases faster than the circuit recovery voltage, the circuit has been interrupted. In an ac circuit the current goes through zero twice each cycle, a phenomenon called the current zero pause. The example in Figure 7-1 has an extremely long zero pause. The dotted line portions of current (I) in the zero pause zone represent the normal current

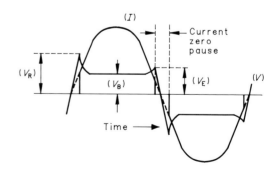

(I) = Arc current
(V) = Arc voltage
(V_R) = Reignition voltage
(V_B) = Burning voltage
(V_E) = Extinguishing voltage

Figure 7-1 AC Arc Current and Voltage Across Arc Plotted Versus Time

waveshape. Figure 7-2 illustrates two examples of reignition voltage versus time. Variations in contact material and size, radiation losses, and other phenomena account for the difference between two interrupting devices. All circuit interrupters depend on the zero pause for circuit interruption whether the medium is air, oil, SF_6, or vacuum. The method is always the same, although the medium and details vary:

- Separate contacts, creating an arc
- Deionized space in the gap during the zero pause to restore high dielectric strength

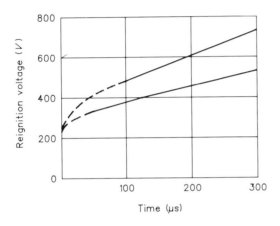

Figure 7-2 *Reignition Voltage for Various Deionizing Times*

AIR-MAGNETIC CIRCUIT BREAKERS

Air-magnetic circuit breakers all depend on one or more of the following principles for operation:

- *Arc Elongation* When the contacts are separated, the arc is progressively elongated as the contacts are drawn apart. Arc elongation results in increased cooling and deionization by diffusion. This causes an increase in the arc burning voltage and in the reignition voltage required at current zero. When a current zero is reached and the dielectric strength of the arc gap exceeds the recovery voltage, the arc is extinguished.

  Arc elongation was the earliest method used for interrupting a circuit. All circuit breakers rely on arc elongation to some extent.

- *Arc Constriction* A much higher voltage is required to maintain an arc in a small hole or narrow slot than is needed to maintain an unconfined arc. The basic structure needed for extinguishing an arc by constriction is

shown in Figure 7-3. Plate 1 is made either of a heat-shock-resistant material, such as ceramic, or an organic material, such as fiber. The arc is initiated at the lower end of the slot and rises or is pushed to the upper slot portion. As the arc rises in the slot, the shape of the slot squeezes or pinches the arc, converting it into a long, thin, low-current arc that is readily extinguished during the zero pause.

- *Arc-restraining Metal Barriers* If an arc is transferred to a series of metal plates (Figure 7-4), the resultant series of arcs will require a higher driving voltage to sustain them. In addition, arc elongation in the individual arcs and the cooling effect of the metal plates combine to effect arc extinction at a current zero. This principle alone is sufficient at relatively low voltages and currents.

- *Magnetic Blowout* Magnetic blowout is any means for magnetically elongating and displacing an arc when the contacts separate (Figure 7-5). Magnetic blowout may be used to create high-speed turbulent motion, causing mixing of the hot arc gases with the surrounding cool air and transferring the arc into arc chutes or metal barriers.

All air-magnetic circuit breakers utilize one or more of these principles. Typical air-magnetic circuit breakers are shown in Figure 7-6.

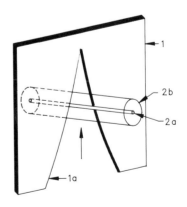

1 = Plate of heat-shock-resistant material
1a = Inverted V-shaped slot
2a = Arc core
2b = Envelope of arc

Figure 7-3 *Barriers With an Inverted V-shaped Slot for Extinguishing Arcs by Constriction*

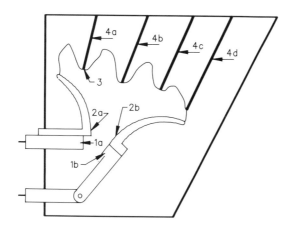

1a, 1b = Main contacts
2a, 2b = Horn—shaped arcing contacts
3 = Arc
4a—4d = Arc—restraining metal barrier

Figure 7-4 Arc-restraining Metal Barriers Subdividing Long Arcs Into Several Serially Related Short Arcs

OIL CIRCUIT BREAKERS

Developed 90 years ago, the oil circuit breaker is the oldest type of power circuit breaker still in use today. Oil circuit breakers are used only for outdoor applications, having been supplanted by air-magnetic (and other) circuit breakers for indoor applications around 1940. Although not readily available in today's domestic market, oil circuit breakers are still in service. An understanding of their operating principles is useful.

Before discussing breaker structures, the properties of insulating oil as an interrupting medium should be considered. All hydrocarbons, including oils used in oil circuit breakers, decompose under extreme heat. The reaction is generally referred to as cracking. By cracking, hydrocarbons of high molecular weight are converted into hydrocarbons of low molecular weight. In the circuit breaker, when the contacts part, the arc immediately vaporizes cracking oil, surrounding the arc with a bubble of vapor and gas.

The cracking process is complex, but the principal gaseous constituents are:

Hydrogen	70%
Acetylene	20%
Methane, carbon dioxide, oxygen, nitrogen	10%

The most significant component in the interrupting process is hydrogen, which is an excellent interrupting medium because it has the property of deionizing arcs at a rapid rate. When the zero pause occurs, the arc energy within the bubble drops to zero. The bubble wall continues to boil releasing more saturated vapor and particles of oil into the residue of the arc. This results in a rapid increase of the reignition voltage of the arc path. Thus, at an early current zero, the arc is extinguished (Figure 7-7a).

Oil Displacement In an oil circuit breaker, when the contacts separate and generate the gas bubble, the gas energetically displaces oil, causing the body of oil above the bubble to rise (similar to the

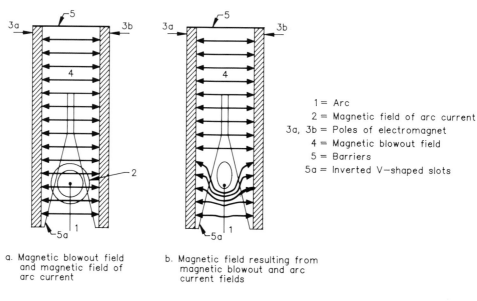

1 = Arc
2 = Magnetic field of arc current
3a, 3b = Poles of electromagnet
4 = Magnetic blowout field
5 = Barriers
5a = Inverted V—shaped slots

a. Magnetic blowout field and magnetic field of arc current

b. Magnetic field resulting from magnetic blowout and arc current fields

Figure 7-5 Magnetic Blowout

reaction from the charge of steam or combustion in an engine). For this reason, the term *oil piston* has been used with reference to the displacement of oil within a breaker tank. The oil-piston effect results in circuit breaker reactions: a downward thrust when the oil piston is accelerated and an upward thrust when it hits the dome of the tank. Circuit breaker reactions may be several times the weight of the breaker and must be accommodated in the foundation or mounting of an oil circuit breaker (Figure 7-7b).

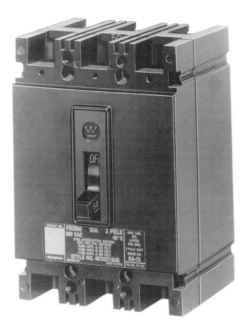

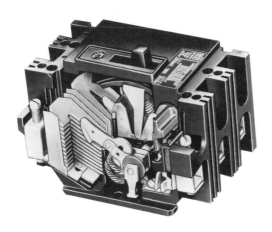

Courtesy of Westinghouse Electric Corp., Beaver, Pa.

Figure 7-6 *Typical Molded-Case Air-Magnetic Circuit Breaker*

Typical Oil Circuit Breakers There are two types of oil circuit breakers.

- *Plain Break-Type Breaker* The plain break-type circuit breaker is the earliest design. It is characterized by limited interrupting capability, high rate of oil carbonization, and high circuit breaker reaction in larger interrupting ratings.

- *Arc-enclosing-Type Circuit Breakers* Later designs used arc-enclosing devices to contain the gas bubble, to increase gas pressure, and to introduce more turbulence in the gas bubble. The results were lower arc energy, less carbonization, faster interruption, and lower circuit breaker reaction, all of which permitted greatly increased interrupting ratings. Low-arc-energy arc-enclosing circuit breakers are referred to by their mode of operation or by trade designations indicating their manufacturers, or both. Such terms are, for instance, Explosion Pot, Deionization Grid, or Ruptor.

The earliest arc-enclosing device, the Explosion Pot, is shown in Figure 7-8. It consists mainly of a strong shell of insulating material.

The design shown in Figure 7-9 is the forerunner of several generations of Ruptor interrupting devices. It differs from the Explosion Pot by having a long throat with a serpentine passage. This permits controlled leakage past the movable contact during interruption.

VACUUM CIRCUIT BREAKERS

The dielectric strength of a vacuum interrupter is not due to slowing of electrons during the zero pause as in other devices but due to no electron collisions occurring in a perfect vacuum. In practice, the vacuum is not perfect; nevertheless, performance is remarkable: a 1-cm gap at 10^{-6} torr will withstand about a 200,000-V peak. In a vacuum, dielectric strength increases only slightly with distance.

When the vacuum circuit breaker is operated, a metallic vapor arc is formed, causing a momentary pressure that may reach several atmospheres. Initially, it is a high-current arc with a single cathode spot emitting large amounts of metal vapor. As the current decreases, the vapor pressure also decreases rapidly because the vapor condenses on the metallic screens. Below a critical value, the arc changes from a constricted discharge with one cathode spot to a diffused discharge with several

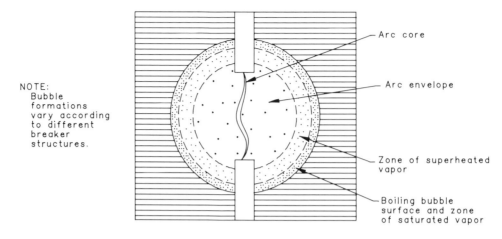

NOTE:
Bubble
formations
vary according
to different
breaker
structures.

Arc core

Arc envelope

Zone of superheated
vapor

Boiling bubble
surface and zone
of saturated vapor

a. Principal constituent parts

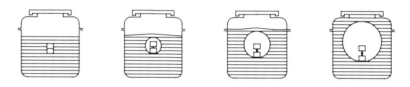

b. Arc bubble growth and displacement of oil, shown
chronologically after separation of contacts

Figure 7-7 *Arc Bubble in a Plain Oil Circuit Breaker*

very small spots that move about rapidly, repelling each other. These small spots have a very high current density and emit streams of electrons without liberating much metal vapor. The interrupter then behaves as a vacuum diode; as current decreases, the electron flow falls to zero, and electrons cease to cross the gap. The inverse voltage strength rapidly increases to a high value as the cool anode is not able to emit electrons, and the circuit is interrupted.

Arc Instability An interesting problem with vacuum interrupters results from arc instability. The diffuse arc is unstable because each spot requires a minimum intensity to emit electrons; below this value it abruptly ceases to operate. This explains the well-known propensity of vacuum equipment to produce overvoltages by current chopping. The problem can be eased principally by the manufacturer's selection of contact material. Test results have shown current chopping in vacuum contactors to range from 0.5 to 5 A and vacuum circuit breakers from 2 to 10 A, depending on contact material. Switching unloaded transformers with vacuum circuit breakers produced overvoltages at 2 to 3.1 per unit. Chopping current for minimum oil, SF_6, and air-blast circuit

breaker types may range from 4 to 20 A. Switching the same unloaded transformers produced overvoltages exceeding 7 per unit. We may conclude that current chopping in vacuum contactors and circuit breakers is not a serious problem when they contain modern suitable contact materials. There are, however, some application areas that require attention when using vacuum equipment (1).

Virtual Current Chopping A reignition in one phase of a three-phase system may induce a high-frequency transient in the other two phases, which may cause the total current in the two phases to pass through zero. It is possible that the current in all three phases will interrupt simultaneously.

Reignition After current interruption, if the transient recovery voltage rises faster than the vacuum interrupter dielectric strength, multiple ignition will occur. All vacuum interrupters are susceptible to multiple reignition irrespective of the chopping current level. The following conditions are vulnerable to multiple reignition:

- A motor with locked-rotor current of 500 A or less switched off during locked-rotor conditions. Motor starting current (locked-rotor current) does not decrease significantly until the motor has achieved perhaps 85% of rated speed.

- Vacuum interrupter contacts separate at a time less than 0.5 ms from natural sinusoidal current zero. This condition may occur 18% of the time on a three-phase system.

- The natural frequency of the transient recovery voltage on the load side of the interrupter is between 0.5 and 5.0 kHz.

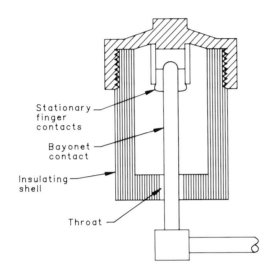

Figure 7-8 *Plain Explosion Pot From Which Arc-enclosing Devices Evolved*

If current exceeds 500 A, or the natural frequency of the transient recovery voltage exceeds 5 kHz, the vacuum interrupter cannot clear the arc at the first current zero, delaying interruption until the next current zero when dielectric strength will be great enough to prevent reignition.

For circuits with a natural frequency of 500 Hz or less, transient recovery voltage rate of rise is low, and reignition is prevented.

If current is less than 20 A, overvoltages are limited to a harmless level.

Protection against overvoltages caused by multiple reignition will also protect against virtual current chopping. Application charts were developed to determine the maximum length of load cable that will not permit multiple reignition for shielded and unshielded cables (Figures 7-10a, 7-10b, and 7-10c [1]). The charts are based on the following equations:

$$L = 2\pi f 3I \quad \text{(Eq. 7-1)}$$

$$C = \ell C_v \quad \text{(Eq. 7-2)}$$

$$f_n = \frac{1}{2\pi(LC)^{1/2}} \quad \text{(Eq. 7-3)}$$

Where:

L = ungrounded motor inductance at locked-rotor condition

f = supply frequency

I = locked-rotor current

C = capacitance of cable

ℓ = cable length

C_v = capacitance per unit length of cable

f_n = natural frequency of the load

Typical vacuum interrupters and vacuum switchgear are shown in Figure 7-11.

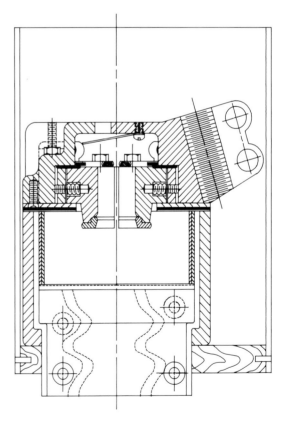

Figure 7-9 *Ruptor Interrupting Device With Serpentine Throat, a Later Version of the Explosion Pot*

SF$_6$ CIRCUIT BREAKERS

SF$_6$ has become the preferred medium for arc interruption by some switchgear manufacturers over the last decade. The reason is the advantageous combination of dielectric, thermal, and arc

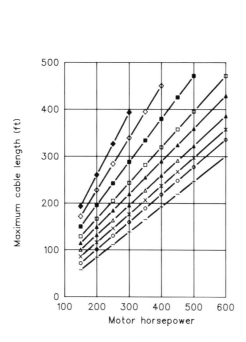

a. Maximum length of shielded cable, 4160 V

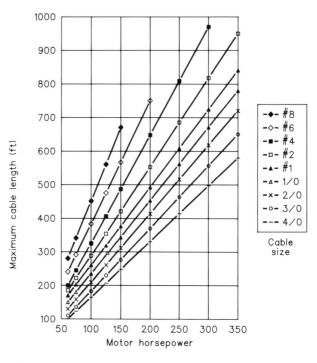

b. Maximum length of shielded cable, 2300 V

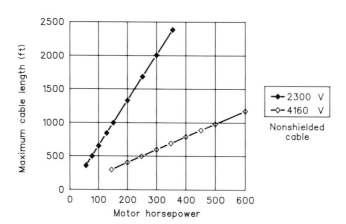

c. Maximum length of nonshielded cable, 2300 and 4160 V, all cable sizes

SOURCE: S. F. Farog and R. G. Bartheld. "Guidelines for the Application of Vacuum Contractors." In *IEEE Transactions on Industry Applications*, vol. 1A-22, no. 1, January/February 1986, p. 105. © 1986 IEEE.

Figure 7-10 *Maximum Allowable Medium-Voltage Cable Length*

extinction properties of the gas. Studies show that transient voltage levels due to current chopping are lower in magnitude than other modern interrupting mediums. Multiple reignitions, with resulting transient overvoltages, are nonexistent with medium-voltage SF_6 interrupters. The pressure of the gas may be continuously monitored, and the breaker may be controlled as a function of the condition of the interrupter. Some SF_6 interrupters can provide significant interruption performance even at zero-gage gas pressure. With special attention given to the types of interrupter envelopes and seals, some SF_6 interrupters are sealed for life and require little or no maintenance throughout their service life.

When an SF_6 circuit breaker is operated and the contacts part, the usual arc is produced. Thermal conductivity of SF_6 is very high, even at elevated temperatures. Thus, when the current is decreasing, the arc temperature drops quickly. Below about $2100°K$, the SF_6 molecules recombine, and

a. Vacuum switchgear lineup

b. Vacuum interrupter (cutaway view)

c. Removable vacuum circuit breaker

Courtesy of General Electric Company, Construction Equipment Business, Burlington, Iowa.

Figure 7-11 Typical Vacuum Interrupters and Vacuum Switchgear

the gas becomes an insulator. This is augmented by free electron capture by fluorine atoms. The circuit interruption occurs at an early current zero. The transient recovery in the region of current zero is slow as compared with other interrupting media. This is an advantage in that an SF_6 interruption is not easily concluded by high-frequency system disturbances. As a result, chop currents are low; and prestrike interruptions, reignitions, virtual chopping, and simultaneous interruptions are practically nonexistent.

The same principles used in air-magnetic circuit breakers may be used in SF_6 breakers with the same results; gas flow and magnetic arc displacement cool the arc, aiding interruption. Because of the nature of the SF_6 gas, wide variations of air-magnetic principles may be employed. The resulting package looks much different and is much smaller than other circuit breakers.

Two designs of SF_6 circuit breakers are currently available in the medium-voltage field:

- *Puffer Type* The puffer design produces gas flow through the arc by displacing a piston, which is attached to the movable contacts. The chamber in which the arc is interrupted is very similar to air-blast circuit breakers. The puffer type is very effective, especially for high interrupting capacities and high-rated continuous currents (ampacities and currents greater than 16 kAIC and 1200 A).

- *Self-extinguishing or Magnetic Type* The self-extinguishing design utilizes magnetic arc rotation and gas flow caused by high temperature in the arcing chamber. The self-extinguishing type is ideally suitable for applications less than 16 kAIC and 1200 A. This type typically has even less current-chopping characteristics than puffer types and is typically used for motor control and low-capacity circuit breakers.

Examples of SF_6 circuit breakers are shown in Figure 7-12.

AIR-BLAST CIRCUIT BREAKERS

As in all compressed gases, compressed air has dielectric strength and thermal properties much greater than those at atmospheric pressure. Compressing air increases the thermal exchange and deionization rates, making it possible to achieve circuit interruption during the current pause, with relatively short arc lengths. All air-blast circuit breakers use air flowing around the arc through a constricting nozzle, which discharges to the

a. SF$_6$ puffer—type pole unit (cutaway view)

b. SF$_6$ removable circuit breaker element (rear view)

Courtesy of Square D. Company, Smyrna, Tenn.

Figure 7-12 *Examples of SF$_6$ Circuit Breakers*

atmosphere. The arc is centered in the nozzle and swept by the air flow, which subjects it to very strong cooling and facilitates deionization and interruption. By choice of air pressure and nozzle design, interrupting capabilities up to 200,000 A at 25 kV or higher can be achieved. Typical air-blast

circuit breakers have a main interrupting chamber for making and breaking load and fault currents and a small auxiliary interrupting chamber that contains contacts in series with a low-ohmic resistor that controls recovery voltage. In operation, the main contacts open and reduce the high-fault or load current to a low current through the low-ohmic resistor. In a few milliseconds, the resistor current is interrupted in the auxiliary chamber.

Air-blast circuit breakers are used principally as generator circuit breakers, and for indoor and outdoor applications at high-continuous current or interrupting ratings. An example of an air-blast circuit breaker is shown in Figure 7-13.

7.4 MEDIUM-VOLTAGE SWITCHGEAR

AVAILABLE EQUIPMENT

Medium-voltage switchgear, nominally rated between 2.5 and 38 kV, is currently available using vacuum, air-magnetic, and SF$_6$ circuit breakers. The majority of power plant applications are at 4.16, 7.2, or 13.8 kV, using vacuum or air-magnetic circuit breakers.

Switchgear is constructed in conformance with American National Standards Institute (ANSI) Standard C37.20-1969/IEEE Standard 27-1974 (2). Medium-voltage switchgear, built as metal-clad, has the following attributes:

- The main switching or interrupting device is of the removable type arranged with a mechanism for moving it physically between connected and disconnected positions and equipped with self-aligning and self-coupling primary and secondary disconnecting devices (most vendors).

- Major parts of the primary circuit are completely enclosed by grounded metal barriers that have no intentional openings between compartments.

- All live parts are enclosed within grounded metal compartments. Automatic shutters prevent exposure of primary circuit contacts when the removable circuit breaker element is in the test position or is removed.

- Primary bus conductors and connections are covered with insulating material throughout.

- Mechanical interlocks are provided to ensure a proper and safe operating sequence.

- Instruments, meters, relays, secondary control devices, and their wiring are isolated by grounded metal barriers from all primary circuit elements with the exception of short lengths of wire as at instrument transformer terminals.

- The door through which the circuit interrupting device is inserted into the housing may serve as an instrument or relay panel and may also provide access to a secondary or control compartment within the housing.

Removable circuit breaker elements are either horizontal draw-out or vertical-lift design. Both are self-aligning and self-coupling. The vertical-lift design is older and was originally designed to directly replace vertical-lift indoor oil circuit breakers.

The principal advantage of vertical-lift equipment is that primary contact separation is clearly visible in the test and disconnected positions. Horizontal draw-out equipment may be easily installed manually as the heavy circuit breaker need not be lifted. Both designs are considered equally acceptable.

A common problem is susceptibility of relays to mechanical shock when mounted on compartment doors. Opening and closing the door may produce sufficient mechanical shock to cause spurious operation of relays. All electromechanical relays, especially those with instantaneous contact elements and some solid-state relays with electromechanical components, are susceptible to varying degrees.

MEDIUM-VOLTAGE SWITCHGEAR COMPONENTS

Major parts of medium-voltage switchgear are:

- *Secondary Enclosure* Located at the front of the unit, this component has a hinged panel with necessary instruments control and protective devices mounted on it. Terminal blocks and some protective devices are mounted within the compartment.

- *Primary Enclosure* The primary enclosure contains high-voltage equipment. It consists of the circuit breaker compartment, bus compartment, cable termination compartment, and auxiliary compartments for voltage (and control power) transformers. Each compartment is separated from the others by metal barriers.

  Interference interlocks are mounted in the circuit breaker compartment to permit only insertion of a circuit breaker with the correct voltage, current, and interrupting ratings.

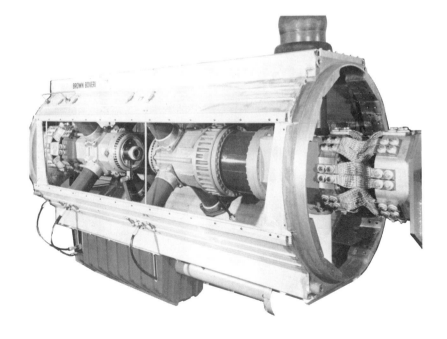

Courtesy of BBC Brown Boveri, Inc., New York.

Figure 7-13 *Example of Air-Blast Circuit Breaker (isolating section open)*

■ *Circuit Breaker Removable Element* This removable circuit breaker, air-magnetic or vacuum type, has a stored energy spring operating mechanism, interlocks, primary and secondary (most vendors) disconnecting devices, antipump relays, and a limited number of auxiliary switches (see Volume 10 for details). The assembly is equipped with wheels for easy movement along the floor.

■ *Auxiliary Switches* Optional circuit breaker and stationary auxiliary switches are available for interlocking and control purposes. Auxiliary switches are Types a and b (see Volume 10 for details): Type a open when the circuit breaker is open, and Type b closed when the circuit breaker is open.

Mechanism-operated Control (MOC) Auxiliary Switches MOC switches are operated directly from the breaker mechanism and are available in the following types:

■ Operate with the circuit breaker in both connected and test positions

■ Operate with the circuit breaker in the connected position only

■ Operate with the circuit breaker in the connected position, but operate with the circuit breaker in the test position if manually selected

A limited number of auxiliary switches are mounted on the circuit breaker removable element, and a larger number (as required) are mounted in the secondary enclosure and linked mechanically to the circuit breaker. Auxiliary switches mounted either on the circuit breaker removable element or in the secondary enclosure may be any of the above types, arranged by either the mechanical linkage or sliding contacts on the secondary coupling.

Truck-operated Contact (TOC) Auxiliary Switches TOC auxiliary switches are mounted in the circuit breaker compartment and operate when the circuit breaker is moved to the operating position. TOC switches may be used for interlocking and remote position indication.

■ *Current Transformers* Current transformers are used to protect personnel and secondary devices from high voltage and to reflect primary current flow in relays, instruments, and meters (see Volume 8).

■ *Voltage (Potential) Transformers* Voltage transformers are used to permit reasonable insulation levels in instrument circuits. They are used for wattmeters and voltmeters and for ground fault detection.

■ *Primary Bus Conductors* The devices connect all units in the switchgear lineup. Primary bus conductors and connections are covered with insulating material throughout.

■ *Automatic Shutters* Automatic shutters cover primary circuit connections when the circuit breaker removable element is in the disconnected, test, and removed positions.

■ *Ground and Test Device* This device is an optional draw-out element that may be inserted into a metal-clad switchgear housing in place of a circuit breaker. It provides access to the primary circuits to permit temporary connections of grounds or testing equipment to the HV circuits. It may be manual, with six bushings for connection to primary circuits, or may include a three-pole, two-position selector switch and stored-energy grounding switch.

SWITCHGEAR RATINGS

Medium-voltage switchgear is rated in selected continuous current steps from 1200 through 3000 A, with short-circuit current ratings from 12 to 48 kA, as shown in ANSI Standard C37.06-1979 (3). Note that manufacturers do not necessarily offer all ratings listed in the ANSI standard, and most manufacturers also have nonstandard circuit breaker ratings, usually with higher close-and-latch capability in selected ratings. Table 2 of ANSI Standard C37.06-1979 lists standard indoor oilless circuit breaker ratings for switchgear.

Salient parts of switchgear circuit breaker ratings are (4):

■ *Rated Maximum Voltage* The rated maximum voltage of a circuit breaker is the highest root-mean-square (rms) voltage, above nominal system voltage, for which the circuit breaker is designed and is the upper limit for operation.

■ *Rated Voltage Range Factor, K* The rated voltage range factor K is the ratio of rated maximum voltage to the lower limit of the range of operating voltage in which the required symmetrical and asymmetrical interrupting capabilities vary in inverse proportion to operating voltage.

■ *Rated Frequency* The rated frequency of a circuit breaker is the frequency at which it is designed to operate. Other frequencies usually require special consideration.

■ *Rated Continuous Current* The rated continuous current of a circuit breaker is the designated limit of current in rms amperes at rated frequency that it will carry continuously without exceeding designated temperature limitations.

■ *Rated Standard Operating Duty* (standard duty cycle) The standard operating duty of a circuit breaker is two-unit close-open (CO) operations with a 15-s interval between operations (CO–15s–CO).

■ *Rated Interrupting Time* The rated interrupting time of a circuit breaker is the maximum permissible interval between energizing the trip circuit at rated control voltage and interrupting the main circuit on all poles when interrupting a current equal to 25% or more of the required asymmetrical interrupting capability at rated maximum voltage.

■ *Rated Permissible Tripping Delay, Y* The rated permissible tripping delay of a circuit breaker is *Y* and is the maximum time that the circuit breaker is required to carry K times rated short-circuit current after closing on this current and before interrupting.

■ *Permissible Tripping Delay, T* Tripping the circuit breaker may be delayed. The rated permissible tripping delay *Y* at lower values of current is in accordance with the following formula:

$$T = Y \left[\frac{\text{K (rated short-circuit current)}}{\begin{array}{c}\text{short-circuit current}\\\text{through circuit breaker}\end{array}} \right]^2 \quad \textbf{(Eq. 7-4)}$$

■ *Rated Short-Circuit Current* The rated short-circuit current of a circuit breaker is the highest value of the symmetrical component of the polyphase or phase-to-phase short-circuit current in rms amperes. It is measured from the envelope of the current wave at the instant of primary arcing contact separation, which the circuit breaker is required to interrupt at rated maximum voltage.

■ *Rated Short-time Current-carrying Capability* The circuit breaker is capable of carrying, for *T*s = 3 s, any short-circuit current the rms value of which, determined from the envelope of the current wave at the time of maximum crest, does not exceed 1.6 K times rated short-circuit current; the maximum crest value of which does not exceed 2.7 times rated short-circuit current; and the rms value (*I*) of which over the 3-s period does not exceed K times short-circuit current.

Symmetrical Versus Total Current Basis of Ratings of Circuit Breakers The original unified series of standards for circuit breakers based on those of American Institute of Electrical Engineers (AIEE) and National Electrical Manufacturers Association (NEMA) and data from the Association of Edison Illuminating Companies and NEMA were developed from 1941 through 1953 and published in the following documents: ANSI Standard C37.4-1953 (*5*), ANSI Standard C37.5-1953 (*6*), ANSI Standard C37.6-1953 (*7*), ANSI Standard C37.7-1952 (*8*), ANSI Standard C37.8-1952 (*9*), ANSI Standard C37.9-1953 (*10*), and ANSI Standard C37.12-1981 (*11*).

In these original standards the basis of the interrupting rating was established as the highest current to be interrupted at the specific operating voltage. It was the rms value, including the dc component at the instant of contact separation, as determined from the envelope of the current wave. Since this method of rating was based on total current, including the dc component, it became known as the total current basis of rating.

Commencing in 1951, the AIEE Switchgear Committee began developing a method of rating based on symmetrical interrupting current. The goals were to simplify application that used high-speed relaying and fast-clearing circuit breakers and to bring American standards into closer agreement with accepted international standards.

The principal change from the total current standard was the basis of rating. The rated short-circuit current was established as "the highest value of the symmetrical component of the short-circuit current in rms amperes," measured from the envelope of the current wave at contact separation, which the circuit breaker is required to interrupt at rated maximum voltage. This rating structure became known as the symmetrical current basis of rating.

The symmetrical current basis of rating group of standards was published in 1964 and consolidated with intervening supplementary standards in 1979 in the following documents: ANSI/Institute of Electrical and Electronics Engineers (IEEE) Standard C37.04-1979 (*4*), ANSI Standard C37.06-1979 (*3*), ANSI/IEEE Standard C37.09-1979 (*12*), ANSI/IEEE Standard C37.010-1979/IEEE Standard

320-1979 (*13*), ANSI/IEEE Standard C37.011-1979 (*14*), and ANSI/IEEE Standard C37.012-1979 (*15*).

In ANSI Standard C37.06-1964 and revisions prior to 1971, circuit breaker *Symmetrical Current* ratings were derived from ANSI Standard C37.06-1961 *Total Current* ratings by a compromise between the asymmetrical current of the former method and the range of related requirements of the new symmetrical method. For a given circuit breaker it is:

$$\begin{matrix}\text{rated symmetrical} \\ \text{short-circuit} \\ \text{current}\end{matrix} = I(1961)$$

$$\times \left[\frac{\text{nominal voltage}}{\text{rated maximum voltage}} \right] F \quad \textbf{(Eq. 7-5)}$$

Where:

$I(1961)$ = symmetrical interrupting rating appearing in ANSI Standard C37.6-1961

F = 0.915 for three-cycle circuit breakers

0.955 for five-cycle circuit breakers

1.0 for eight-cycle circuit breakers

It must be stressed that this numerical conversion must be approved by the manufacturer, as noted in the ANSI standards.

For circuit breakers still in use rated on a total current basis, the existing standards ANSI Standard C37.4-1953, ANSI Standard C37.6-1953, ANSI Standard C37.7-1952, and ANSI Standard C37.9-1953 will continue to be applicable. Circuit breakers are no longer manufactured to the total current basis (asymmetrical) standards.

Example 1 *Replacement of Old Circuit Breaker With a Modern One*

An old indoor oil circuit breaker has seriously deteriorated and must be replaced because it has been out of production for decades and replacement parts are unobtainable. The power system has not been altered, so we are sure that available short-circuit current is unchanged. It will be replaced with a modern breaker, but a conversion must be made from the old total current basis to the newer symmetrical current basis to place the order, since no equipment is now manufactured to the old basis.

The rating nameplate on the old circuit breaker gives the following information:

Rated kV: 4.16 kV

Maximum kV: 4.76 kV

Interrupting amperes at rated voltage: 12 kA

Continuous current: 1200 A

MVA 100

Interrupting time: five cycles

Substituting and calculating as in Equation 7-5:

$$I \text{ symmetrical} = 12 \text{ kA} \left[\frac{4.16 \text{ kV}}{4.76 \text{ kV}} \right] \times 0.955$$

$$= 10.015 \text{kA}$$

Thus, any circuit breaker rated greater than 10 kA symmetrical interrupting current at 4.76 kV and having a V/k voltage less than 4.16 kV will be a satisfactory substitute.

If the system has changed, thus increasing available short-circuit current, and new equipment is to be added, the application guide ANSI Standard C37.010-1979/IEEE Standard 320-1979 (*13*) gives the calculation procedures.

APPLICATIONS AND RELATED REQUIREMENTS

Medium-voltage switchgear is used to feed loads throughout the plant, usually secondary unit substations and large motors that are not cycled frequently. Medium-voltage switchgear is available, as applicable, from 2.4 through 38 kV. Historically, the trend has been to use higher-voltage systems. Currently power plant electrical systems use 4.16-, 7.2-, and 13.8-kV class medium-voltage switchgear. (See Volume 3, *System Planning*.)

Equipment may be selected based on load requirements and available short-circuit currents. Circuit breakers may be used for motor starting, applied on motors with full-load current up to the circuit breaker continuous current rating. Because power systems continue to grow, even after the equipment is purchased and installed, it is advisable to be on the conservative side in ampacity and short-circuit ratings. Methods of calculating short circuits and applying circuit breakers are delineated in ANSI Standard C37.010-1979/IEEE Standard

320-1979. Volume 3 also discusses sizing medium-voltage circuit breakers.

Most electrical equipment, such as motors, buses, and transformers, may be temporarily overloaded, and there may be some resultant acceptable reduction in useful life. Circuit-breaker continuous-load current may be increased based on low ambient temperature or increased from a low-current load for an allowable time based on maintaining the same hot-spot temperature, which does not constitute an overload condition.

Circuit breakers may also carry load currents higher than permitted by ambient compensation for emergency load periods, which may cause a reduction in operating life of the equipment. ANSI Standard C37.010-1979/IEEE Standard 320-1979 (13) and Supplement b (16) give overload and emergency-load-carrying capability.

Exceeding interrupting ratings and related capabilities (without the manufacturer's consent) may result in circuit breaker failure to interrupt, probably catastrophically.

If the interrupting ratings and related capabilities of a circuit breaker are exceeded, for example, because of substitution of a lower impedance transformer or changes in the system, the following changes must be made to correct the situation:

- Change the system to reduce available short-circuit current; divide the system into smaller units (see Volume 3).
- Add lumped impedance (reactors) to reduce short-circuit current.
- Replace circuit breaker(s) with higher interrupting rated circuit breakers.

Transient Recovery Voltage Transient recovery voltage is the voltage that initially appears across the open poles of a circuit breaker immediately after the arc is extinguished. Following current zero, the voltages on both sides of the circuit breaker recover to their driving source voltages. The circuit breaker is stressed by the voltage difference between both voltages. For successful interruption, the breakdown voltage of the circuit breaker must always exceed the recovery voltage.

Transient recovery voltage requirements for medium-voltage switchgear are not currently (1985) defined in the standards, but the IEEE Switchgear Committee will incorporate them in the near future. There have been suspected cases of transient recovery voltage failures of 15-kV class switchgear (17); however, transient recovery voltage problems are usually associated with transmission line switching—systems with considerable distributed

inductance and capacitance. ANSI/IEEE Standard C37.011-1979 (14) presents more discussion and calculation procedures.

Capacitive Current Switching Breakers used for capacitive current switching require careful consideration. For single-shunt bank or back-to-back switching, it will usually be conservative to use 1.25 times the nominal capacitor current at rated capacitor voltage for ungrounded neutral operation, or 1.35 times the nominal current for grounded neutral operation, for calculating required breaker ampacity. Note that not all circuit breakers have back-to-back switching capability. Only circuit breakers specifically manufactured for back-to-back switching are so rated (3).

Complex capacitor switching requires further analysis. Refer to ANSI/IEEE Standard C37.012-1979 (15) and the vendor for calculation methods and recommendations.

Repetitive Duty Circuit breakers should not be used for repetitive duty, such as motor starting. If the circuit breaker is cycled more than once a day, it may be worn out or will require major maintenance every two or three years. Circuit breakers are usually not designed for highly repetitive duty. Repetitive duty such as motor starting is better served by using medium-voltage motor starters.

7.5 SECONDARY UNIT SUBSTATIONS

Secondary unit substations have a medium-voltage to low-voltage transformer, and a lineup of low-voltage switchgear mechanically and electrically coupled. A double-ended substation has two unit substations with a tie circuit breaker between the two low-voltage switchgear sections. Secondary unit substations are fed from medium-voltage switchgear at 2.4 to 13.8 kV. When two unit substations are fed from the same circuit breaker, a load break switch is frequently used as an isolating means. The transformer is usually a three-phase unit, transforming the 5- to 15-kV primary voltage to distribution voltage levels, which may be 120 through 600 V. The most commonly used distribution voltage is 480 V. The low-voltage switchgear section feeds motor control centers and other large unit loads and motors of perhaps 100 to 200 hp, which are not frequently cycled. Low-voltage switchgear used today is invariably comprised of air-magnetic circuit breakers.

INCOMING LINE SECTION

When one secondary unit substation is fed from a medium-voltage circuit breaker, the incoming line is usually connected directly to the medium-voltage to low-voltage transformer. When two or three secondary unit substations are fed from one medium-voltage circuit breaker, the incoming line is usually connected to an unfused air load–interrupter switch. The air-interrupter switch provides an isolating means so that one secondary unit substation may be deenergized without deenergizing others connected in parallel.

The load-interrupter switch has a quick-make, quick-break spring operating mechanism and switch element capable of making and latching fault current and breaking full-load current. Load-interrupter switches are available in ratings of 600 and 1200 A, 2.4 through 38 kV, with momentary ratings up to 80 kA, and fault closing ratings up to 61 kA.

Disconnecting switches will also be found without arc-interrupting devices, capable of interrupting only negligible current. They must be interlocked with the main circuit breaker in the low-voltage switchgear section of the secondary unit substation, so that the disconnect switch will be required only to interrupt magnetizing current to the secondary unit substation transformer. When purchasing new equipment, a user should give preference to a load interrupter switch rather than a disconnect (magnetizing current) switch to eliminate interlocking requirements. Indeed, the cost of interlocks will probably exceed any savings that result from omission of arc interrupting devices.

TRANSFORMERS

A secondary unit substation transformer is typically rated between 225 and 3000 kVA, three-phase, 2.4 to 13.8 kV primary to 208 to 600 V secondary. Volumes 2 and 3 discuss transformers in more detail. There are seven kinds of transformers in three categories in use, although some are used infrequently:

- *Oil-immersed Transformers* The oldest and least expensive design transformers use mineral oil and paper insulation in a sealed tank. They are entirely satisfactory for outdoor installations and chemically active environments. Indoor applications of oil-filled transformers are restricted due to fire code requirements. Indoor application requires installation in a vault, an expensive and inconvenient structure.

- *Less-Flammable Liquid Transformers* Until recently, this category of transformer was filled with askarels, synthetic halogenated hydrocarbons containing polychlorinated biphenyls (PCBs) as coolants. PCBs are no longer acceptable because they are not 100% biodegradable. Currently, less-flammable liquid transformers are filled with polydimethylsiloxane (also called dimethyl silicone or silicone fluid) or processed hydrocarbons.

  Less-flammable liquids are defined as having a fire point not less than 300°C. Installation requires liquid containment in a noncombustible building, liquid containment and an automatic fire extinguishing system, or a vault in a combustible building. Insurance companies may require additional protection in a combustible building.

- *Nonflammable Liquid Transformers* A nonflammable transformer is defined as having no flash point, no fire point, and being nonflammable in air. When rated 35 kV and lower, such transformers may be installed indoors without restrictions.

  Two fluids are currently in use in the nonflammable category:

  - *Perchloroethylene* (Cl_2:CCl_2), also known as ethylene tetrachloride, tetrachloroethylene, Perclene, Perk, and Wecosol. Perchloroethylene is a colorless liquid with an etherlike odor. It is an excellent solvent and is widely used in the dry-cleaning and metal-degreasing businesses. It is a relatively safe fluid to use and has a long history of safe use in the dry-cleaning and chemical industries. It is, however, moderately toxic and requires proper handling for complete safety.

    Perchloroethylene is moderately toxic by ingestion, with a probable lethal dose between 1 oz and 1 pt for a 150-lb man (500 mg/kg body weight).

    Overexposure to perchloroethylene vapors will result in headaches, confusion, nausea, and lack of coordination. Extreme overexposure could result in severe personal injury or death. Adequate ventilation must be maintained if perchloroethylene vapor is liberated.

Extremely high vapor concentrations may occur in emergency situations and in confined or poorly ventilated areas.

Perchloroethylene vapor is six times heavier than air and may accumulate in low areas, presenting danger of asphyxiation.

In the presence of fire or electric arcing, perchloroethylene can decompose to form carbon dioxide (CO_2), hydrogen chloride (HCl), chlorine (Cl), and phosgene or trichloroacetic acid. Phosgene gas is colorless and has the odor of new-mown hay or green corn (*18*). It is a severe respiratory irritant, causing coughing and nose and throat irritation from a minute or so of low concentration exposure (0.1 to 5 ppm). Brief exposures to 50-ppm concentrations may be fatal. There may be no immediate warning that dangerous concentrations of the gas are being breathed. Trichloroacetic acid is corrosive and irritant to the skin, eyes, and mucous membranes. When responding to fires or electric arcing, firefighters should assume that hydrogen chloride and possibly phosgene or chlorine may be present. Note that presence of hydrogen chloride or chlorine, which are sharply irritating, is not sufficient to warn of the presence of high levels of phosgene. It is possible to be exposed to toxic levels of phosgene before irritation indicates an existence of a problem.

EPRI EL-4407 (*19*) discusses the maintenance and handling of perchloroethylene-filled electrical equipment in more detail.

□ *Trichlorotrifluoroethane* ($C_2Cl_3F_3$), also known as R-113, Refrigerant 113, and Freon 113, is used in vapor-cooled transformers. It is a colorless liquid with a slight etherlike odor. Trichlorotrifluoroethane and other fluorocarbons have relatively low toxicity compared with most chemicals but require proper handling for complete safety.

Trichlorotrifluoroethane vapor is six-and-a-half times heavier than air and can cause suffocation by reduced oxygen available for breathing (simple asphyxiation). Breathing high concentrations of vapor may cause light-headedness, narcosis, cardiac irregularities, unconsciousness, or death. Decomposition by high temperatures (open flames, glowing metal surfaces, arcing)

forms hydrogen fluoride (HF), hydrogen chloride, and possibly carbonyl halides. The decomposition products are much more toxic than the parent fluorocarbon but are also strongly irritant. It is most difficult to remain voluntarily in the presence of the decomposition products at concentrations where physiological damage occurs (*20, 21*).

When handling trichlorotrifluoroethane, smoking and use of space heaters should be prohibited, and good ventilation should be maintained.

■ *Ventilated Dry-Type Transformers* Early dry-type transformers were constructed of the same materials used in other electrical apparatus and were designed for 55°C rise (105°C temperature class). Later, as higher-temperature insulating materials were developed, transformers were rated at 80°C rise (150°C temperature class), 115°C rise (185°C temperature class), and most recently, 150°C rise (220°C temperature class). Transformers are sometimes designed to the earlier temperature ratings using high-temperature (220°C) materials and restricting the rise to 80°C or 115°C when a more conservative rating is required. Dry-type transformers are preferred for indoor installations because there is no fluid to burn or leak and there are no prohibitive restrictions. Maintenance is merely occasional cleaning. Note that standard dry types have three deficiencies:

□ They have reduced basic impulse insulation level (BIL) and may require surge suppressors on the high-voltage windings in special applications.

□ The insulation is hygroscopic and susceptible to chemically active environments. The windings must be acceptably dry before energizing and can be a problem in high-humidity environments and seasonal energizations.

□ Clean filtered air is required to maintain cleanliness.

■ *Totally Enclosed Nonventilated Dry-Type Transformers* The totally enclosed nonventilated type has no openings to allow entrance of surrounding air and solid contaminants and particles in the atmosphere. It is designed for installation indoors and outdoors in moderately contaminated industrial environments.

■ *Sealed Dry-Type Transformers* This type of transformer has a dry-type core and coil assembly in a sealed tank, filled with a nonflammable gas. The gas is commonly hexafluoroethane (F_3CCF_3, also called Freon 116, perfluoroethane, and carbon hexafluoride) or nitrogen (N_2). These gases are benign compared with most chemicals, but precautions should be taken in event of a large gas spill. Hexafluoroethane has the same characteristics as other fluorocarbons as noted under trichlorotrifluoroethane, and nitrogen is, of course, a simple asphyxiant.

Because the transformer assembly is isolated from the external environment, sealed dry-type transformers may be applied in all environments. Because the gas meets the definitions of a nonflammable fluid, transformers can be applied without restrictions. Sealed dry-type transformers may be used advantageously in areas that require explosion-proof equipment.

■ *Cast-Coil and Encapsulated-Coil Transformers* Cast-coil and encapsulated dry-type transformers have their coils cast or encapsulated in epoxy or polyester resins. They are impervious to moisture and most chemical environments. Cast-coil and encapsulated-coil transformers are considered nonflammable and are recommended for indoor and outdoor installations for all but extreme environments. Extreme environments would be excessive dust or dirt that could clog cooling ducts, corrosive contaminants that could attack exposed conductors, and conducting contaminants that could promote tracking failures.

Transformers 501 kVA and larger may be furnished with forced-cooling fans, giving additional forced-cooled capacity of 15 or 25% for oil-filled and silicone-liquid-filled units, 33% for ventilated dry types, and 50% for cast-coil and trichlorotrifluoroethane-filled vapor-cooled units.

Table 7-1 presents the approximate cost of transformers relative to the lowest-cost oil-filled unit.

Choosing the optimum transformer type is not a simple problem. The installed cost of the lowest-cost oil-filled unit can easily exceed more expensive types when vaults, fire protection, and liquid-containment costs are added. Environmental constraints, such as a corrosive atmosphere or high humidity, may rule out ventilated dry types and perhaps even cast-coil transformers.

Table 7.1 Comparative Cost of Transformers

Transformer Type	Percent
Oil-filled	100
Silicone-liquid-filled	130
Nonflammable liquid-filled	140
Ventilated dry-type	
150ºC 60–kV BIL	125
150ºC 95–kV BIL	140
80ºC 60–kV BIL	135
80ºC 95–kV BIL	150
Totally enclosed nonventilated dry-type	160
Cast-coil dry-type	190
Sealed dry-type	250

Selecting the lowest cost transformer option involves three categories:

■ Acquisition cost
■ Installation cost
■ Present value of annual costs

Selecting the lowest-cost transformer can be done by calculating installation cost plus present value of the annual cost:

1. Calculate total losses at the expected load (L_{EL}).

$$L_{EL} = L_c + (L_T - L_c)F^2 \qquad \textbf{(Eq. 7-6)}$$

Where:

L_{EL} = total transformer losses at the expected load

L_c = core losses, vendor data, remains constant at all loads (no load loss)

L_T = total winding losses at full load, vendor data

F = fraction of 100% load expected on the transformer

2. Calculate annual operating cost (C_o).

$$C_o = L_{EL} \times H \times D \times C_E + \text{annual insurance} + \text{maintenance} \qquad \textbf{(Eq. 7-7)}$$

Where:

C_o = total annual operating cost

L_{EL} = total transformer losses at expected load

H = hours per day transformer operates

D = days per year transformer operates

C_E = energy cost, \$/kW

3. Calculate present value of total annual operating cost (C_{pv}). C_{pv} is needed to calculate the amount of money required today to pay for transformer operation over its life.

$$C_{pv} = C_o \times \frac{(1 + i)^N - 1}{i(1 + i)^N}$$ **(Eq. 7-8)**

Where:

C_{pv} = present value of total annual operating cost

C_o = total annual operating cost

i = rate of return

N = years of postulated transformer life

4. List installed transformer cost (C_I), which is the sum of purchase price, shipping cost, insurance, warranty, price escalation, labor, materials, field supervision, and field testing.

5. Calculate total transformer cost (C_T)

$$C_T = C_I + C_{pv}$$ **(Eq. 7-9)**

Where:

C_T = total transformer cost

C_I = installed transformer cost

C_{pv} = present value of total annual operating cost

LOW-VOLTAGE SWITCHGEAR

Low-voltage switchgear, nominally rated between 208 and 600 Vac, is currently available only as air-magnetic circuit breakers. The majority of applications are at 480 or 600 Vac.

Low-voltage switchgear is constructed in conformance with ANSI Standard C37.20-1969/IEEE Standard 27-1974 (2) as metal enclosed and is completely enclosed on all sides and top with sheet metal (except for ventilating openings and inspection windows) containing primary power circuit switching or interrupting devices, or both, with buses and connections, and may include control and auxiliary devices. Access to the interior of the enclosure is provided by doors or removable covers. The reader is invited to compare the attributes of metal-clad versus metal-enclosed switchgear. Metal-clad switchgear has all high-voltage parts separately enclosed and insulated, and low-voltage wiring and devices may not even be exposed to high-voltage.

Metal-enclosed switchgear need only be enclosed on all sides and top with sheet metal. It need not be compartmented, its bus need not be insulated, and low-voltage components and wiring may be exposed to it.

Note that metal-enclosed construction is used up to 1000 V, and metal-clad construction is used above 1000 V; thus, the method of construction is appropriate to the risks. Modern switchgear has been designed for maximum safety of operating personnel under normal conditions, excluding internal switchgear failures.

The low-voltage power circuit breakers are contained in individual grounded metal compartments and controlled either remotely or from the front of the panels.

The circuit breakers are horizontal, draw-out removable and are self-aligning and self-coupling. Low-voltage circuit breakers use series-current tripping and thus do not require external control power for overcurrent tripping operation. External control power will be required for electrically operated breakers (for closing spring charging) and for shunt trip devices (for remote closing and tripping).

Major parts of low-voltage switchgear are:

- *Bus Compartment* Located in the middle of the unit, horizontal and vertical bus connects all equipment in the unit. Low-voltage bus is not normally insulated but may be as an option. Metal barriers between the bus and rear field cable terminations are also optional.

- *Circuit Breaker Enclosures* Each circuit breaker is individually metal enclosed. Primary disconnect shutters may be optionally available.

- *Circuit Breaker Removable Element* The removable circuit breaker is an air-magnetic type with a stored energy spring-type operating mechanism. It may be either manually operated or electrically operated. The trip unit may be either electromechanical or solid-state, with short time delay, long time delay, and instantaneous-trip functions. Circuit breakers may have integrally mounted current limiting fuses to extend short-circuit current ratings up to 200 kAIC.

- *Shunt Trip* A shunt trip provides for remote electrical tripping of a circuit breaker. It may be controlled by a switch, push button, or protective relays.

- *Undervoltage Trip* Optional undervoltage trip protects against severe undervoltage by automatically tripping the circuit breaker. An undervoltage trip device picks up at approximately 85% of bus voltage and trips the circuit breaker between 30 and 60% of bus voltage. An optional time delay to trip is available to eliminate nuisance tripping during transients.

- *Key Interlocks* Circuit breakers have a provision for a key interlock that may be required to ensure correct sequence of operations.

- *Auxiliary Switches* Optional circuit breaker auxiliary switches are available for interlocking and control purposes. Auxiliary switches are Types a and b: open when the breaker is open, and closed when the breaker is open, respectively.

- *Voltage Transformers* Voltage transformers are used to permit reasonable insulation levels in instrument circuits. They are used for wattmeters, voltmeters, and ground fault detection.

- *Operations Counter* An operations counter is optional on low-voltage breakers.

- *Bell Alarm With Lockout* An optional bell alarm switch operates a and b contacts. It operates when the circuit breaker is tripped automatically (any means other than manual trip button or shunt trip). The contacts may be used for remote alarm of an automatic trip. The lockout feature mechanically locks the circuit breaker open upon automatic tripping and must be manually reset.

- *Electric Lockout* An optional electric lockout device electrically interlocks breakers so that two cannot be closed at the same time.

- *Remote Close Solenoid for Manually Operated Breaker* This option provides a means to electrically close a manual circuit breaker from a remote location. The circuit breaker must be charged manually.

- *Solid-State Trip Device Test Set* A portable instrument for field-checking all solid-state trip device functions and calibration.

Low-voltage circuit breakers may be furnished with series-current limiting fuses to extend short-circuit interrupting ratings to 200,000 A symmetrical.

Representative examples of low-voltage switchgear are shown in Figure 7-14.

LOW-VOLTAGE SWITCHGEAR RATINGS

Low-voltage switchgear is rated from 225 through 4000 A, 14,000 through 200,000 rms symmetrical ampere interrupting rating in conformance with ANSI Standard C37.16-1980 (22). The 200-kA ratings are attainable only with current-limiting fuses. Note that manufacturers do not necessarily offer all ratings listed in the ANSI standards, and some manufacturers have some nonstandard circuit breaker ratings, usually with higher ampacity and interrupting ratings. However, the 225-A frame size is not currently in production, and the 600-A frame size is becoming obsolete. ANSI Standard C37.16-1980 lists low-voltage switchgear ratings. Salient parts of the switchgear ratings (23) are:

- *Rated Maximum Voltage* The rated maximum voltage of a circuit breaker is the highest rms voltage, three phase or single phase, at which it is designed to perform. Rated maximum voltages are 635, 508, and 254 V. For fused circuit breakers, the 635-V rating becomes 600 V to match the fuse rating.

- *Rated Frequency* Rated frequency is the frequency at which the circuit breaker is designed to operate. Rated frequency is 60 Hz.

- *Rated Continuous Current* The rated continuous current of a circuit breaker is the rms current at rated frequency that it will carry without exceeding designated temperature limitations. The rated continuous current of a circuit breaker equipped with direct-acting trip devices or fuses with a rating lower than the frame size is limited to the rating of those devices.

- *Rated Short-Time Current* For an unfused circuit breaker, the rated short-time current is the current at which it is required to perform its short-time current duty cycle (two periods of ½-s current flow, separated by a 15-s interval of zero current) at rated maximum voltage under prescribed test conditions. This current is the rms symmetrical

a. Secondary unit substation with high—voltage load—interrupter switch,
liquid—insulated transformer, and low—voltage switchgear section

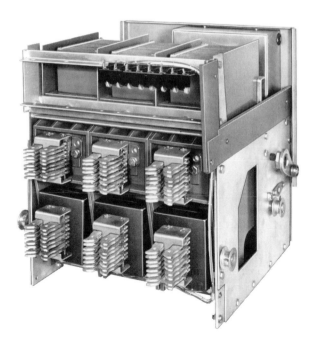

b. Low—voltage circuit breaker (rear view)

Courtesy of Westinghouse Electric Co., St. Louis, Mo.

Figure 7-14 Representative Examples of Low-Voltage Switchgear

value measured at one-half cycle after short-circuit initiation. Fused circuit breakers do not have a rated short-time current because the fuses will blow. Only the circuit breaker element of a fused circuit breaker assembly has a rating as described above.

- *Rated Short-Circuit Current* The rated short-circuit current uses either unfused circuit breakers or fused circuit breakers.

  □ *Unfused Circuit Breakers* The rated short-circuit current of an unfused circuit breaker is the current at which it performs its short-circuit current duty cycle at rated maximum voltage under prescribed test conditions. This current is the rms symmetrical value measured one-half cycle after short-circuit initiation.

  □ *Fused Circuit Breakers* The rated short-circuit current of a fused circuit breaker is the current at which it performs its short-circuit current duty cycle under prescribed test conditions. The short-circuit duty cycle consists of an O (open) followed by a CO (close-open) operation. The time between O and CO operations is that time necessary to replace fuses and reset the open-fuse trip device. This current is the rms symmetrical value measured one-half cycle after short-circuit initiation.

- *Rated Control Voltage* The rated control voltage is the voltage at which the mechanism of the circuit breaker is designed to operate when measured at the power terminals of the operating mechanism with highest current flowing. Rated control voltages and voltage ranges are listed in ANSI Standard C37.16-1980 (*21*).

Circuit breakers are selected to have interrupting ratings greater than the short-circuit current available at the switchgear bus. In determining suitability for system conditions, consideration should be given to:

- Source contribution
- Motor contribution
- System power factor
- Type of operating mechanism
- Duty cycle
- Type of trip devices

Guidance in calculating short-circuit currents is given in ANSI/IEEE Standard C37.16-1980 (*22*),

IEEE Standard 141-1976 (*24*), IEEE Standard 241-1983 (*25*), IEEE Standard 242-1975 (*26*), and Volume 3.

Note that all circuit breakers, whether used as main, feeder, or tie circuit breakers, must meet the same short-circuit current requirements. Application of switchgear circuit breakers above their short-circuit current ratings in cascade is not recommended.

APPLICATIONS AND RELATED REQUIREMENTS

Low-voltage switchgear is used to feed loads grouped near the secondary unit substation. The loads are low-voltage motor control centers (perhaps two per feeder circuit breaker), and low-voltage motors rated perhaps 100 hp or larger. Circuit breakers may be selected based on full-load ampacity of the connected loads. Motor starting current may be disregarded as the rating structure recognizes this use, and the circuit breakers will withstand motor starting current without harm.

As indicated earlier, circuit breakers should not be used for repetitive duty (for example, motor starting), because they may wear out or require excessive maintenance in two or three years. Motor starters and contactors are more suitable for repetitive operations.

ANSI/IEEE Standard C37.16-1980 (*22*) gives circuit breaker ratings in horsepower for motor starting.

Example 2 *How to Select Circuit Breakers*

A secondary unit substation with a 1000-kVA, 13.8- to 480-V transformer provides a short-circuit current capability of 25,000 A, including motor contributions at the switchgear low-voltage bus. How do we select circuit breakers?

- *Main Circuit Breaker* Full-load current is 1203-A self-cooled or 1603-A fan-cooled. A 2000-A circuit breaker with interrupting rating above 25 kA will be acceptable.

- *Circuit Breaker Size Required to Control a 200-hp Induction Motor* The motor full-load current is 240 A. Any breaker with full-load ratings equal to or greater than 240 A and 25,000 A short-circuit current is acceptable. The lowest available current rating is 800 A, providing a generous margin.

■

7.6 MOTOR CONTROL

LOW-VOLTAGE MOTOR CONTROL

Low-voltage motor control equipment in generating station auxiliary systems is usually a motor control center wherein motor starters are combined in plug-in units in vertical assemblies. Standard sizes and types are defined in NEMA Industrial Controls and Systems series standards: NEMA Standard ICS 1-1983 (27), NEMA Standard ICS 2-1983 (28), NEMA Standard ICS 4-1983 (29), and NEMA Standard ICS 6-1983 (30).

A combination motor controller unit includes an externally operable circuit disconnecting means, circuit overcurrent protection, and a magnetic motor controller with associated auxiliary devices when required (NEMA Standard ICS 2-1983, Sect. 322.02 [28]).

A control power transformer may be furnished to operate at 120 V for control circuits, rather than the supply voltage that may be 480 or 600 V. This practice eliminates the safety hazard of having high voltages, perhaps 480 or 600 V, in control circuits of control boards.

Feeder tap units include an externally operable means for circuit disconnection and branch-circuit overcurrent protection, principally used for nonmotor loads.

Motor control centers are defined in terms of class and type in NEMA Standard ICS 2-1983, Sect. 322 as follows:

- *Class I* Class I motor control centers consist of a mechanical grouping of combination motor control, feeder tap assemblies, and other units arranged in a convenient assembly. They include connections from the common horizontal power bus. They do not include interwiring or interlocking between units or to remote devices and do not include system engineering.

- *Class II* Class II motor control centers consist of a grouping of combination motor control, feeder tap assemblies, and other units designed to form a complete control system. They include electrical interlocking and interwiring between units and to remote devices, including connection to the common power bus.

Class and Type of Motor Control Center Motor control centers are manufactured to the following classes and types with the following features:

- Class I, Type A
  - No terminal boards for load or control connections.
  - Connection diagrams only for each combination controller or control assembly.
  - Sketches of the overall dimensions of the control centers.

- Class I, Type B
  - Unit control terminal boards are provided. Load terminal boards are provided for combination starters size 3 or smaller. Terminal boards are mounted on or adjacent to each unit. No load terminal boards are provided for feeder trip units.
  - Connection diagrams only for each combination controller or control assembly.
  - Sketches of the overall dimensions of the control centers.

- Class I, Type C
  - Master section terminal boards, including load terminals for combination controllers size 3 or smaller, and all control terminals for all combination controllers or control assemblies in each vertical section are mounted on the stationary structure. Also, complete wiring is provided between combination controllers or control assemblies and their master terminal boards. No load terminal boards are provided for feeder tap units.
  - No wiring between sections or between any master terminals.
  - No interconnecting between any combination controllers or control assemblies. All outgoing wires from any unit will be carried to the master terminal board, except wiring for combination controllers size 4 or larger.
  - Connection diagram for each combination controller or control assembly.
  - Sketch of main terminal boards showing general location of terminals.
  - Sketches of the overall dimensions of the control centers.

- Class II, Type B
  - Unit control board provided. Unit load terminal blocks provided for combination controllers size 3 or smaller. Terminal boards are mounted on or adjacent to each unit. No load terminal boards are provided for feeder tap units.

□ Necessary interconnecting wiring between combination controllers and control assemblies in the same or other sections.

□ A connection diagram of the complete control assembly.

□ Sketches of the overall dimensions of the control centers.

Figure 7-15 shows types of motor control centers and components.

COMBINATION MOTOR CONTROLLER RATINGS

Motor controllers are horsepower rated, depending on the application. Controllers should not be used with motors whose full-load current or horsepower rating exceed the continuous current or horsepower ratings given in the NEMA ICS standards. The ultimate trip current of overcurrent relays or other motor protective devices should not exceed the service-limit current rating of the controller.

Motor Control—The Problem Defined The paramount problem in motor control is providing protection for the motor under all operating conditions: starting and running. A motor is unique in that the starting current is perhaps six times the full-load running current for a time duration of several seconds. Protection can easily be provided for either condition (with a standard fuse, for example) but cannot cover both conditions: If the fuse is selected for running protection, it will blow on starting; if selected for starting protection, it provides inadequate running protection. Short-circuit current protection must also be provided, which may be 1000 times motor full-load current.

Motor Control—The Solution

■ Motor protection

□ *Fuses* One-element fuses are now available that have time-current characteristics providing starting, running, and short-circuit current protection. However, they do not provide single-phasing protection in the event of fuse failure and do not coordinate with all motors. Dual-element fuses are not widely used for motor protection in power plant electrical systems.

□ *Thermal Relays* Because overcurrent is the major cause of motor overheating, it follows that devices designed to protect motors from excessive heating would sense current

in one way or another. The majority of overload relays in use today are thermal devices that rely on the line current flowing to a motor for the heating effect. To protect a motor properly, they should possess thermal characteristics closely resembling those of the motor: Figure 7-16 compares the thermal characteristics of a typical motor and typical overload relay. These curves show that the overload relay will trip (disconnect the motor from the line) just before motor overheating for all values of excessive load current. Higher current not only causes motor overheating to take place in a shorter period of time but also causes earlier tripping of overload relays. This is characteristic of inverse time relays.

□ *Melting-Alloy Relays* Melting-alloy overload relays (Figure 7-17) consist of a heater element, eutectic alloy, alloy pot, ratchet wheel, pawl, spring, and contacts. The intensity of heat dissipated by the heater varies directly with the line current and acts upon the eutectic alloy (alloy with a precise low melting point). The spring-loaded pawl operates the contacts in such a manner that the contacts are forced open unless the pawl is held in place. This is the function of the ratchet wheel; it secures the pawl and thus forces the contacts closed. Because the shaft of the ratchet wheel is secured by the solidified eutectic alloy, the contacts remain in the closed position. However, should the motor draw excessive current for a long enough period of time, the heat dissipated by the heater will melt the eutectic alloy, allowing the ratchet wheel to spin. The spring-loaded pawl is then free to move, allowing the contacts to open, which, in turn, de-energizes the control circuit and drops out the starter. After the alloy has cooled and hardened, the unit can be manually reset.

□ *Bimetallic Relays* Figure 7-18 illustrates the principle of the bimetallic overload relay. This type of overload relay also contains a heater that is sensitive to line current. As the line current increases and the heater dissipates more heat, a bimetallic strip is heated instead of a eutectic alloy. This bimetallic strip is designed to flex a predetermined distance when it reaches a specific temperature. The temperature corresponds

a. Typical motor control center

b. Removable combination starter with control power transformer

Courtesy of Square D Company, Burlington, Iowa.

Figure 7-15 Motor Control Centers and Components

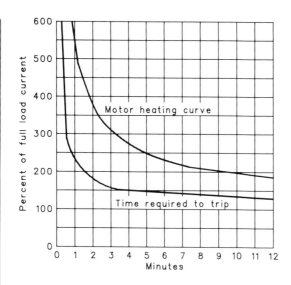

Figure 7-16 *Comparison of Thermal Characteristics of a Typical Motor and Typical Overload Relay*

to the point at which the motor should be disconnected from the line to avoid excessive heating. When the bimetallic strip bends this predetermined distance, force is applied to the contact mechanism, and the contacts open to disconnect the motor from the line.

Compared with the melting-alloy overload relay, the bimetallic overload relay has both advantages and disadvantages. One advantage is the ability of most bimetallic units to be converted from the manual reset to automatic and vice versa by merely moving a spring or lever. However, this apparent advantage also leads to a pitfall. Overload relays should normally be of the manual reset type to call attention to an overheating motor in order to locate the trouble. It is easy for a busy maintenance man to set an overload of this type to automatically reset itself, so that he is not bothered. The motor problem thus remains

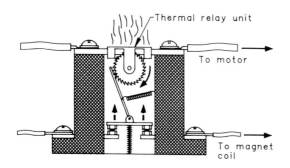

Figure 7-17 *Melting-Alloy Overload Relay*

unsolved and causes unnecessary motor deterioration. Another danger is the possibility of an overload relay being set to automatically reset itself on a two-wire control scheme where personnel injury could result from a motor suddenly starting without warning. The automatic reset feature does have its place, however, protecting a motor that is isolated, such as in an oil field where personnel would be required to travel a considerable distance to reset the device, or controlling equipment, such as a refrigerator where it would be more desirable to deteriorate the motor than to have it disconnected from the line until personnel are in attendance. Disconnection could result in loss of the refrigerated goods.

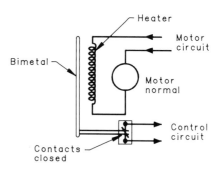

a. Normal position

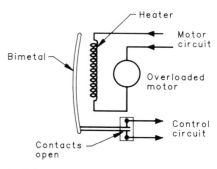

b. Tripped position

Figure 7-18 *Bimetallic Overload Relay*

A second advantage of most bimetallic overload relays is the incorporated adjustment. This allows the trip point to be set from approximately 85 to 115% of the rated ultimate trip current.

Most bimetallic overload relays also have removable interchangeable heater elements, permitting easy changes of current rating without removing the entire thermal relay.

□ *Thermal Overload Relay Class Descriptions* Overload relays are classified by time-current characteristics, designated by a class number indicating the maximum time in seconds at which it will function (trip) when carrying 600% of its current rating. A class 10 relay will function (trip) in 10 s or less, class 20 relay in 20 s or less, and class 30 relay in 30 s or less.

A class 20 overload relay is appropriate for the vast majority of applications. A class 10 relay is appropriate for specialized motors with a low thermal time constant, and a class 30 relay is appropriate for slow-starting loads.

□ *Thermal Relay Ambient Temperature Sensitivity* Thermal relays, being temperature-operated devices, are all somewhat sensitive to ambient temperature. As ambient temperature increases, thermal relay sensitivity increases (lower trip current). This increase is not a drawback because it roughly parallels thermal capability of the motor at higher temperature. If ambient temperature is over the standard 40°C (up to 50°C), or the motor is in a cooler ambient than the thermal relay, ambient-compensated thermal relays can be used. Ambient-compensated thermal relays have a substantially flat temperature coefficient up to 50°C.

■ Short-circuit protection

□ *Fuses* Historically, fuses were the first devices used for short-circuit protection and are a viable option today. Current-limiting fuses have the advantage of interrupting capability up to 200 kA. When used, fuses will be mounted in a fusible switch to provide an interrupting means. Fuses have the disadvantage that one may fail (open) causing single phasing, which may cause motor failure.

□ *Circuit Breakers, Thermal Magnetic* Thermal-magnetic circuit breakers were the first circuit breakers to be used in combination motor starters. When used in a combination motor starter, a thermal-magnetic circuit breaker is used for short-circuit protection only. The thermal trip level is above the thermal relay setting in the combination starter and is either redundant or affords no protection to the motor if the thermal relay fails to operate. Further,

because thermal-magnetic circuit breakers come in discrete ratings, mostly nonadjustable, there is the possibility of a gap in protection between the locked-rotor current and short-circuit current levels. Thermal-magnetic circuit breakers are available as an option today but are not recommended without extenuating circumstances.

□ *Circuit Breakers, Motor Circuit Protector* The magnetic-only motor circuit protector was devised around 1960, specifically for use in combination motor starters. It has continuously adjustable trip levels, permits close coordination with the motor, and permits the combination starter to provide completely coordinated protection from full-load current up to bolted fault current. All manufacturers of circuit breaker–type combination starters currently use magnetic-only circuit breakers. Magnetic-only circuit breakers are recommended.

□ *Contactors* Each combination starter contains a power contactor that provides motor starting and stopping (on and off). These rugged devices will provide trouble-free service for perhaps 200,000 full-load operations. The contactor is designed to interrupt overloads only and will not interrupt short-circuit currents, which are higher than the overload currents.

□ *Control Power Transformers* Power line voltage can be used for control power (contactor energization and indicator lamps) in a starter if the control conductors do not exit the cabinet. If the control conductors do exit the cabinet, a lower control voltage is advisable for safety, and control power transformers are recommended. Standard control power transformers have a 120-V secondary, which is the best choice between reliability and safety. Minimum control power transformer size is generally two and one-half times the contactor sealed voltampere rating as an industry standard. It is best to err on the high side to permit use of auxiliary relays and devices and allow use of longer control cables. When long control cables are used, an interposing relay may be used to eliminate voltage drop in the contactor circuit. This is especially true for NEMA size 3 and larger starters.

Control power transformers can be furnished in each individual starter, or one large control power transformer can furnish control power to a lineup of starters. Both schemes are satisfactory, but individual control power transformers provide greater system reliability. If a single large control power transformer fails or a protective fuse blows, the entire motor control center is out of service. Conversely, with individual control power transformers, only one starter is out of service.

□ *Motor Control Center Application* For typical wiring diagrams and control schemes, see Volume 10. For overload relay applications and circuit coordination, see Volume 8.

MEDIUM-VOLTAGE MOTOR CONTROL

Medium-voltage motor controllers comprise disconnecting means, current limiting fuses, contactor, current transformers, and protective relays. A control power transformer is also usually provided. Controllers are made to meet two classes of performance (NEMA Standard ICS 2-1983, Sect. 324 [28]).

- Class E1 controllers employ their contactors for both starting and stopping the motor and for interrupting short-circuit currents or fault currents exceeding operating overloads.

- Class E2 controllers employ their contactors for starting and stopping the motor and employ fuses for interrupting short-circuit currents or fault currents exceeding operating overloads.

Ratings Medium-voltage motor controllers are available in various motor ratings up to 8000 hp and 7200 V. Standard ampacity ratings are 180 A and 360 A, and nonstandard ratings are available up to 800 A.

Components Medium-voltage motor controllers contain the same components as low-voltage motor controllers, except medium-voltage circuit breakers are not used. All medium-voltage controllers have the following components.

- *Disconnecting Means* A nonload breaking disconnecting switch is provided to isolate all components for maintenance. It provides a visible break and shutters to isolate the energized bus contacts when open.

- *Current-limiting Fuses* Current-limiting fuses are provided for short-circuit protection.

They are mounted in a readily accessible area for easy replacement. An available option is an anti-single-phasing trip bar. The bar is activated by a blown fuse on any phase and immediately trips the contactor to shut down the motor.

- *Contactor* The contactor may be air magnetic or vacuum interrupting. Both are acceptable. The air-magnetic contactor is easier to inspect and evaluate, but the vacuum-interrupting contactor will require less maintenance. Note that there is no need for concern about current chopping with vacuum contactors. The propensity to current-chop depends on vacuum contact or contact material. Material that vaporizes easily under arcing reduces the propensity to current-chop and is used in vacuum contactors.

- *Contactor Operating Mechanism* Contactor operating mechanisms are of two types: electrically held and mechanically latched. The electrically held mechanism that drops out (opens the contactor) in event of loss of voltage or severe undervoltage, is appropriate for most applications. Mechanically latched mechanisms are for use when the contactor must stay closed during severe undervoltage or loss-of-voltage conditions. Examples would be fire pumps, transformer feeders, capacitor bank switching, and loads where the motor is more expendable than the function of equipment being served.

- *Current Transformers* These are used to isolate the protective relays from high voltages and high currents.

- *Protective Relays* Optional protective relays applicable to medium-voltage motor controllers are:
  □ Thermal eutectic and bimetallic thermal overload relays
  □ Standard electromechanical relays
  □ Solid-state relays that give protection including:
    1. Overtemperature (RTD) protection
    2. Overtemperature/overcurrent protection
    3. Open-phase and phase reversal protection
    4. Open-phase and phase unbalance protection
    5. Ground-fault protection
    6. Overcurrent protection
    7. Annunciation and alarm functions

Volume 8 discusses protective relays and their applications.

■ *Control Power Transformer* A fused control power transformer is furnished to provide power to the contactor and ancillary devices.

Medium-voltage controllers are built into structures nominally 90 in. high and may be bused together in lineups and with other equipment.

7.7 PANEL BOARDS

Lighting and distribution panel boards are built in conformance with NEMA Standard PB 1-1984 (*31*). They are wall or flush mounted for power distribution near the loads served. They may be single-phase, two- or three-wire, or three-phase, three- or four-wire. Bus ratings are 50/110/225/400/800 A, and the number of feeds varies from 6 to 60. Input to the panel board may be through lugs, a thermal-magnetic molded-case circuit breaker, a nonautomatic switch, or a fused switch. Feeder devices may be either thermal-magnetic molded-case circuit breakers or fused switches, either plug-in or bolt-in construction. Panel board bus may be either aluminum or copper, usually tin-plated.

MOLDED-CASE CIRCUIT BREAKERS

Molded-case circuit breakers are rated and tested to NEMA Standard AB 1-1975 (*32*). Their full rating is achieved in free air. Thus, when mounted in an enclosure (panel board or motor control center), they must be derated or applied at no more than 80% of their free air rating, unless the circuit breaker is clearly marked 100% rated.

Circuit breakers may be field-tested per NEMA Standard AB 2-1976 (*33*) for function. Note that this test is not a calibration test; it merely verifies circuit breaker function. Verifying circuit breaker calibration in the field is difficult, especially at higher currents, because the calibration is sensitive to waveform variations.

Ordinarily, molded-case circuit breakers in panel boards should be rated to interrupt the short-circuit current available at the panel board bus. However, if the feeder and main circuit breakers have been qualified as a group in cascade, lower-rated circuit breakers may be used. When rated in cascade, the circuit breaker need only interrupt the let-through current.

Molded-case circuit breakers are sealed devices. They cannot be disassembled and worked on.

When performance is unsatisfactory or contact resistance is too high, they should be discarded and replaced. Molded-case circuit breakers should be mechanically operated periodically to prevent seizure of parts. Additionally, some have a test button to exercise the trip unit, which should be beneficially exercised at the same time.

7.8 DC EQUIPMENT

Dc equipment is used in power plant auxiliary service systems to provide independent control power to switchgear and other equipment and for dc motors used in critical applications requiring an independent power source. Dc systems comprise a storage battery (discussed in Volume 9), low-voltage switchgear, motor control equipment, and panel boards. Dc systems are invariably 125 or 250 V (nominal) for power plant equipment.

DC LOW-VOLTAGE SWITCHGEAR

Dc low-voltage switchgear will be identical to ac low-voltage switchgear with two exceptions:

■ Dc circuit breakers will be identical in construction to ac circuit breakers, except the middle pole may be omitted.

■ Dc circuit breakers will, of necessity, have electromechanical trip units. (Solid-state trip units use current transformers as sensors and for power; however, they do not work on dc.)

Dc switchgear is applied as battery circuit breakers and distribution circuit breakers, never for motor starting. Full-voltage motor starting for dc motors is limited to about 1½ hp because of excessively high starting current; thus dc switchgear is too large and is an inappropriate use.

Dc switchgear has the same features as ac switchgear:

■ Electromechanical trip unit with short-time delay, long-time delay, and instantaneous functions

■ Shunt trip, for remote electrical tripping of the circuit breaker

■ Undervoltage trip, for protection against severe undervoltage

■ Key interlocks, to ensure correct sequence of operations

- Auxiliary switches, for interlocking and control purposes
- Bell alarm with lockout, used for remote alarm and lockout upon automatic trip
- Electric lockout for electrically interlocking circuit breakers so that two cannot be closed at the same time
- Remote-close solenoid for manually operated circuit breaker to provide a means for closing a manual circuit breaker from a remote location

Dc switchgear is typically rated 25,000- or 50,000-A short-circuit current at 250 Vdc, three-cycle interrupting time (60-cycle basis).

DC LOW-VOLTAGE MOTOR CONTROL

Dc motor control equipment may be furnished as motor control centers or may be separately mounted when required. Dc motor control centers will have the same class and type designations as listed in Section 7.6.

Short-circuit protection and disconnecting means will be provided by either:

- Fuses in a fusible switch.
- Thermal-magnetic molded-case circuit breaker. (Note that magnetic-only motor circuit protectors have no published dc ratings.)

Overload and starting protection will be provided by thermal-overload relays, either bimetallic or melting-alloy types.

A dc contactor will be provided for starting operations.

The following optional components are available:

- Start-stop push-button station
- Forward-reverse-stop push button station
- Hand-off–automatic selector switch
- Indicating lights
- Line ammeter
- Dc voltmeter
- Elapsed-time meter

Full-voltage starting is normally limited to NEMA size 1 starters with a maximum of 1½-hp, 125-V motor load. Starting resistor sizes and accelerating points should be recommended by the vendor and approved by the user. Reduced-voltage, reversing starters should be supplied with holding coils and commutating field-discharge resistors for use when the motor decelerates.

SPEED CONTROL

Dc motors are designed to achieve rated speed and horsepower with full line voltage applied across the (shunt) field. If this type of operation is planned, no field control components are required.

If speed control by field weakening is required, the speed range must be stipulated when the *motor* is purchased (although all dc motors can have speed control by field weakening, to some extent). For speed control by field weakening, additional starter components are required:

- *Speed Range 2:1* Full field relay and field rheostat
- *Speed Range Greater than 2:1* Field accelerating relay and field rheostat

The field rheostat is customarily furnished by the purchaser and installed in the starter by the vendor, if supplied in sufficient time. It may be the hand-adjustable, flat-plate type or a fixed type.

DC PANEL BOARDS

Dc panel boards may be mounted integrally with a dc motor control center or may be separately mounted. They are the dead-front safety type, equipped with thermal-magnetic circuit breakers or fused switches. Note that when molded-case circuit breakers are applied on dc, the interrupting ratings are substantially less than for ac, typically one-half to one-third of the ac interrupting ratings.

7.9 GENERATOR CIRCUIT BREAKERS

HISTORY AND APPLICATIONS

Early power station designs used generator circuit breakers to connect either to the station bus or to the main transformer, which connected to the high-voltage transmission system. The generator circuit breaker was used for synchronizing and for all routine switching and clearing of a fault within the generator unit (Figure 7-19). Note that this arrangement still finds application in hydro-generating stations, pumped-storage stations, and in other applications where multiple generators are tied to a single step-up transformer.

By the 1950s, generator size had increased beyond available switchgear capability, and the unit-connected generator became standard. In the unit-connected arrangement, the generator is connected

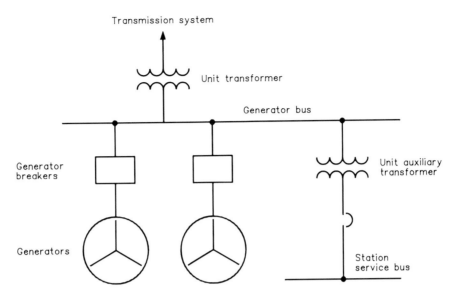

Figure 7-19   *Generating Station With Generator Circuit Breakers*

directly to the main transformer, and a high-voltage circuit breaker is used for synchronizing and switching operations (Figure 7-20). Off-site power is brought in through a station service (startup) transformer for startup and is transferred to the station auxiliary transformer when the generator has been synchronized and connected to the system.

However, generator circuit breakers are available today that will match the capabilities of the largest available generators. They are costly and have found application principally in nuclear power stations. Nuclear power stations are required to have two independent off-site power sources to ensure capability for safe shutdown and public safety. Without a generator circuit breaker, this requirement is met by using two station service transformers fed by two independent power lines (Figure 7-21).

Using a generator circuit breaker permits back-feeding through the main transformer with the generator circuit breaker open; thus, the main

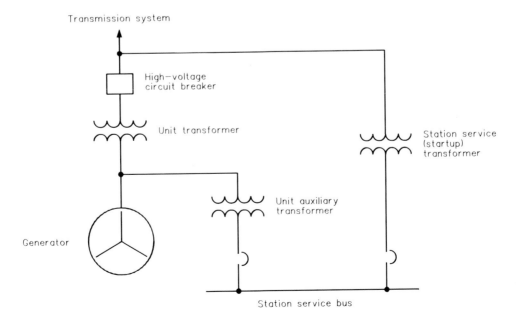

Figure 7-20   *Generating Station With Unit-connected Generator*

transmission line is available as an off-site source. This permits deletion of the second station service (startup) transformer and second independent high-voltage line (Figure 7-22). Elimination of the second station service transformer and second independent line represents a substantial savings over the cost of a generator circuit breaker. For further discussion, refer to IEEE Standards 765-1983 and 308-1980.

The case for applying generator circuit breakers in fossil fuel plants is less compelling. With the generator circuit breaker open, one can backfeed through the unit transformer for startup power, thus eliminating the station service transformer. However, in event of failure of the unit auxiliary transformer, no power will be generated until it is replaced, which may take several months. Thus, for reliability and continuity of service, a station service transformer is highly desirable, even with use of a generator circuit breaker (Figure 7-23).

AVAILABLE EQUIPMENT

Various comparable ratings are available up to:

Load current	48 kA
Maximum rated voltage	36 kV
Symmetrical interrupting current	275 kA
Closing capability	750 kA crest

Several permutations of components are available to provide different levels of interrupting capability.

Load Break Switch The load break-switch configuration may be used to switch normal generator current for startup and synchronizing, and other functions, but has no substantive short-circuit current-interrupting capability. Faults must be interrupted by the high-voltage circuit breaker in the

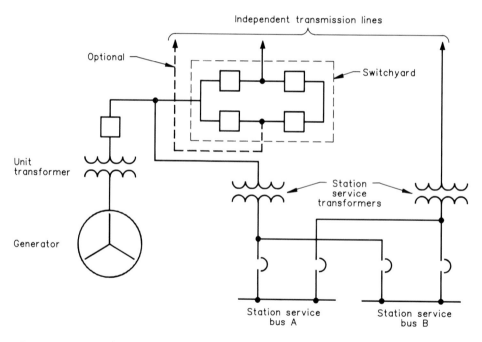

Figure 7-21 *Nuclear Generating Station, Unit-connected With Two Station Service Transformers*

step-up transformer circuit. Note that this provides no protection from generator short-circuit current contributions to faults in the step-up and station service transformers. The generator short-circuit current contribution has a long time constant and contributes significantly to the damage in event of an internal transformer failure.

Medium-Fault Interrupting Capability Medium-fault interrupting capability permits isolation of the generator from a step-up or station service

transformer or bus fault but will not interrupt the system short-circuit current in event of a generator fault.

High-Fault Interrupting Capability This arrangement imposes no limits to the short-circuit protection system, permitting simplicity and flexibility in the protection system.

Operation of generator circuit breakers is different from most circuit breaker applications. In contrast to circuit breakers on air-insulated overhead

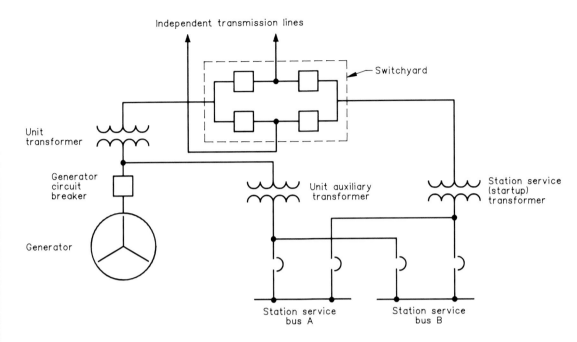

Figure 7-22 Nuclear Generating Station With Generator Circuit Breaker

lines, where fault current paths can usually be considered self-breaking, generator breakers are tripped open in case of faults and are not reclosed until the cause of the fault is determined and repaired or isolated.

7.10 BUS

There are three types of bus in use:

- *Nonsegregated-Phase Bus* A nonsegregated-phase bus is one in which all phase conductors are in a common metal enclosure without barriers between phases (Figure 7-24a).

- *Segregated-Phase Bus* A segregated-phase bus is one in which all phase conductors are in a common metal enclosure but are segregated by metal barriers between phases (Figure 7-24b).

- *Isolated-Phase Bus* An isolated-phase bus is one in which each phase conductor is enclosed by an individual metal housing and separated from adjacent conductor housings by an air space (Figure 7-24c).

CONSTRUCTION FEATURES

Bus conductors may be bars, channels, angles, rounds, squares, or hexagonals. They may be copper or aluminum. They may be bare or insulated throughout. Bus conductors are usually plated at bolted conducting joints.

Bus enclosures may be fabricated from aluminum or steel. Aluminum enclosures must be used above 2000-A bus ratings to avoid hysteresis losses present in steel. Enclosures may be ventilated or nonventilated, indoor or outdoor, and may be rated "proof" or "tight" against rain or dust and other contaminants. Wind loading and ice loading may be required. Service conditions will dictate which type of bus structure is required.

BUS RATINGS

Electrical bus is rated similarly to its connected equipment, including the following items:

- *Rated Voltage* The rated voltage of a bus structure is the highest nominal system voltage at which it is designed to operate.

- *Rated Frequency* The rated frequency of a bus structure is the frequency at which it is designed to operate.

- *Rated Continuous Current* The rated continuous current of a bus structure is the current in amperes at rated frequency that it will carry continuously without exceeding the limit of specified temperature rise.

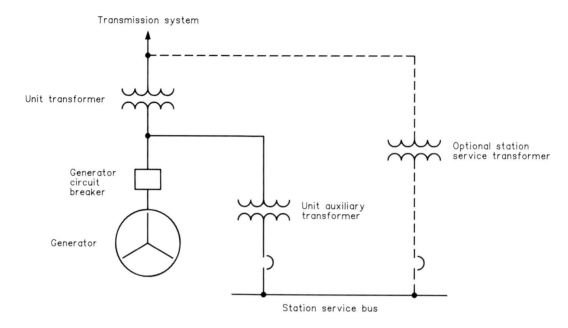

Figure 7-23 *Fossil Fuel Generating Station With Generator Circuit Breaker*

■ *Rated Momentary Current* The rated momentary current of a bus structure is the rms total current that the bus structure will be required to withstand.

■ *Withstand Test Voltage* A withstand test voltage is a voltage that a bus structure must withstand without flashover or other electrical failure when the voltage is applied under specified conditions. Low-frequency voltages are expressed as volts rms for a specific time, and impulse voltages are expressed in crest voltage of a specific wave.

Consideration of the solar radiation effect on outdoor sections is recommended. Note that solar radiation may typically add 15°C rise to outdoor sections (34). A sunscreen may be added to eliminate solar heating effects when they are excessive.

NONSEGREGATED-PHASE BUS

Nonsegregated-phase bus is available with ratings up to 10,000 A, 5- through 34.5-kV, 80-kA short-circuit current. This bus enclosure, both ventilated or nonventilated, is available for indoor and outdoor applications. Nonsegregated-phase bus is used to connect the station service transformer and startup transformer to medium-voltage switchgear. It also may be used as the generator leads from small power plants.

Nonsegregated-phase bus may have heaters to prevent condensation and wall brackets and vapor barriers where the bus passes through external building walls.

SEGREGATED-PHASE BUS

Segregated-phase bus may be used where space limitations prevent use of isolated-phase bus. It has substantially the same flux-neutralizing characteristics as isolated-phase bus but higher losses because of unfavorable geometry. It gives much greater protection from phase-to-phase faults than nonsegregated-phase bus and is useful when high momentary currents and impulse voltages may be found.

ISOLATED-PHASE BUS

Stray-Flux Problem Isolated-phase bus has evolved over the last 50 years in response to the stray-flux problem. As generator size increased, generator lead current increased. At 8000 A and above, stray flux can result in heating of steel members in proximity to the bus, such as building steel, reinforcing bars in concrete, pipe hangers, gas and water pipes, cable trays, ladders, railings, platforms, and other components. Temperatures achieved due to stray flux will not be high enough to affect structural strength or combustibility but are a serious safety problem. The

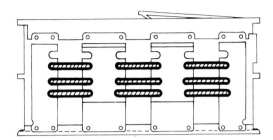

Application: Used to connect transformers to
switchgear, for tie connections between motor
control centers and large motors, and as the
main generator leads in small generator
and hydro plants.

Conductors: Copper or aluminum, insulated.

Supports: Standard fiberglass.

a. Nonsegregated—phase bus

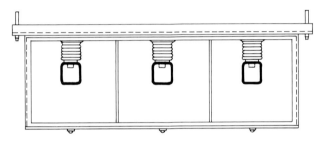

Application: Used as generator leads in
power plants, switchgear tie—in in
metal—enclosed substations, and in factories.

Conductors: Copper or aluminum.

Supports: Fiberglass or porcelain.

b. Segregated—phase bus

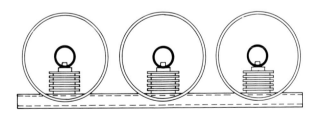

Application: Used primarily as the main
generator leads in power plants.

Conductors: Copper or aluminum.

Supports: Fiberglass or porcelain.

c. Isolated—phase bus

Nonsegregated-phase bus as manufactured by Delta-Unibus
Corporation, Cleveland, Ohio.

Figure 7-24 Bus Types

building steel, cable trays, ladders, and other components are usually in a relatively inaccessible location, and a workman grasping an unexpectedly hot surface may instinctively let go and fall. (Note also that the standards permit metal bus enclosures to reach 80°C when easily accessible and 110°C when unaccessible.) Bus structures are expected to be warm and, thus, are not a problem (Section 8, Table 14 of ANSI Standard C37.20-1969/IEEE Standard 27-1974 [2]).

Noncontinuous-Enclosure Design The noncontinuous-enclosure design was first used in 1937. Each phase conductor is enclosed by an enclosure that is grounded at one end and insulated at all other places (Figure 7-25a). A common ground is carried the length of the bus assembly.

In the noncontinuous design, each phase current produces random currents in the other phase enclosures (but not in its own enclosure), the effect of which is to weaken the magnetic field considerably inside the bus enclosures. The result is that electromagnetic forces on insulators and conductors are reduced by as much as 90% of the forces that would result if the enclosures were not present.

Although the noncontinuous design gives excellent shielding against electromagnetic forces, the external magnetic field is not greatly attenuated. Tests have shown that the external magnetic field will be about 70% of the field due to the unshielded conductor current, still requiring magnetic shielding to reduce heating in nearby steel members. Also, there is a voltage rise on the enclosure, about 2 V at the ungrounded end for normal load currents; however, voltage can be dangerously high under short-circuit conditions.

Continuous-Enclosure Design The problems enumerated above led to the continuous-enclosure design, which was first used in 1968. Each phase enclosure is continuous throughout, with welded cross-connection plates at the ends (Figure 7-25b). The continuous-enclosure design need only be grounded at one place but is most commonly grounded at both ends. It does not require insulation at intermediate support points.

In the continuous-enclosure design, each phase conductor current induces a current opposite in direction and nearly equal, in its own phase enclosure the return path being the other phase enclosures and end plates. This current neutralizes flux from the phase conductor, with the result that external flux is approximately 5% of that

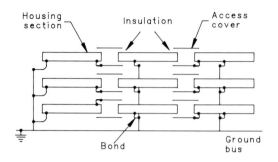

a. Noncontinuous

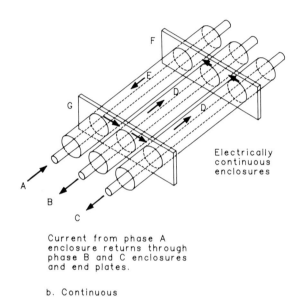

b. Continuous

Current from phase A enclosure returns through phase B and C enclosures and end plates.

Figure 7-25 *Isolated-Phase Bus Enclosure Designs*

which would exist if the enclosures were not present. Induced heating problems are absent, and only mechanical clearance is required for nearby structural members. An additional benefit from the continuous-enclosure design is approximately 93% reduction in electromagnetic forces on conductors and insulators.

Table 7-2 summarizes the electromagnetic forces and stray-flux heating from the various designs of isolated-phase bus.

Bus Cooling Isolated-phase bus may be self-cooled or force-cooled. The choice is primarily economic, depending on bus ampacity and length. An economic evaluation must be made of the losses' first cost. Also, operating requirements versus time and temperature characteristics of the bus must be considered.

Table 7.2 Electromagnetic Forces and Stray-Flux Heating From Isolated-Phase Bus

Isolated-Phase Bus Comparison	Unshielded Conductor (%)	Noncontinuous Design (%)	Continuous Design (%)
Electromagnetic forces on bus	100	10*	7*
External magnetic flux	100	70	5
Stray-flux heating	100	50	1

*Depends on dc component

For example, a self-cooled 25,000-A bus would probably not be economical unless very short. Conversely, a force-cooled 12,000-A bus would probably not be economical unless exceedingly long, due to the incremental cost of the cooling unit. Below 14,000 A, the bus savings for forced cooling are minimal and easily eclipsed by the cost of the cooling unit.

In event of loss of cooling air, bus conductor and enclosure temperature will sharply rise well above allowable temperatures. To prevent this, load current must be reduced to the self-cooled rating. How much time is available for orderly load reduction depends on the self-cooled rating and the initial temperature of the bus. If the time interval is insufficient, a lower self-cooled rating is applicable. To eliminate this problem, redundancy may be built into the cooling package. At the least, a spare mounted motor may be provided. Many modern power plants provide 100% redundant cooling packages.

Three General Arrangements of Forced-Cooling Systems

- *End-fed* Air is admitted to the center-phase enclosure at the generator and flows to the transformer termination, where it divides and returns to the cooler through the two outer-phase enclosures (Figure 7-26a).

- *Center-fed* When air velocity for proper cooling becomes too high (over 40 mph), air is admitted halfway between the generator and transformer (Figure 7-26b). The quantity of air required is the same, but velocity is cut in half. Pressure drop is reduced, and less horsepower is required for the fan.

- *One-Way* If the above systems are insufficient, then air flows one way. Air is admitted to each phase at the generator and returned to the cooler from the transformer end (Figure 7-26c).

When the generator is hydrogen cooled, there is danger of hydrogen leakage from the bushings into the bus cooling system; however, seal-off bushing may be provided at the generator terminals. The generator bushings and terminals must still be cooled, so air from the supply duct is introduced into the generator termination compartment through dampers and discharged to the atmosphere. Hydrogen detectors may be placed near the bushings to give an alarm in the event of hydrogen leakage. An alternative is placing hydrogen detectors near the generator bushings (with no seal-off bushings) and changing the cooling system to once-through operation upon a hydrogen leak alarm to prevent hydrogen buildup in the cooling system.

The basic cooling system consists of a single fan with drive, water, air-to-water heat exchanger, and makeup filter. An additional damper and air duct to the atmosphere may be added for once-through operation in the event of loss of cooling water or hydrogen alarm (Figure 7-27).

It is recommended that the forced-cooling system on isolated-phase bus be run even when the bus is not in use, in order to preclude condensation in the bus.

ISOLATED-PHASE BUS ACCESSORIES

The following accessories are commonly furnished with an isolated-phase bus:

- *Voltage Transformers and Surge Protection* Integrity of the isolated-phase construction continues into surge protection and voltage transformer cubicles. Each surge protector and voltage transformer is mounted in an individual-phase compartment and is connected to the main bus by isolated-phase bus.

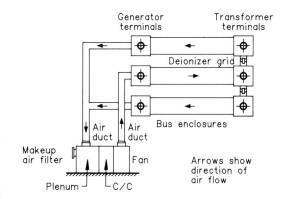

a. End—fed

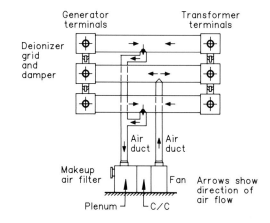

b. Center—fed

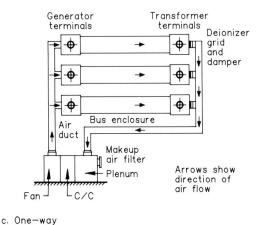

c. One—way

Figure 7-26 Forced-Cooling Systems

■ *Neutral Grounding Equipment* Generators are usually high impedance grounded through a transformer and loading resistor or a reactor.

The equipment is mounted in a metal enclosure with a bus duct section connected to the generator terminator enclosure.

■ *Sealing Bushings* As noted, these components may be used as a hydrogen seal or as a seal to the station service transformer bus tap. The isolated-phase tap bus feeding the station service transformer has low capacity requirements and does not require forced cooling. A small amount of cooling air is continually bled into the tap bus to prevent condensation.

■ *Thermometers* Thermometers may be placed on the bus conductors and viewed through windows in the bus enclosures to check bus conductor temperature.

■ *Wall Frame and Support Plate* Used where isolated-phase bus passes through the building wall to outdoors.

■ *Disconnecting Links* Used at the generator or transformer ends to provide isolation for

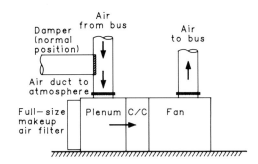

a. Normal operation — air recirculated

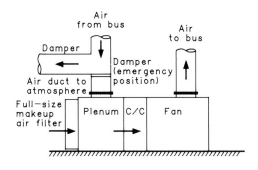

b. Emergency operation — air circulated once and exhausted to the atmosphere

Figure 7-27 Cooling System Operation

testing. The open gap with links removed shall be large enough to provide safe isolation from energized sections.

- *Telescoping Disconnecting Switches* Used in lieu of disconnecting links. At high ampacities, removing disconnecting links may take an unreasonable time.

- *Transformer Adapter Hoods* A set of three hoods to seal off the bus when the transformer is out of service.

- *Bushing Enclosures* For generator and transformer, including flexible boots.

- *Cooling Package* Consists of a fan belt driven by a motor, a heat exchanger with cooling coils, return air plenum, fresh-air filters, dampers, return air duct, vibration boots, and all associated equipment.

- *Crossover Ducts and Dampers* At the generator and transformer as needed, including air ducts, air control baffles, deionizing baffles, and thermostat on the bus enclosures as required.

- *Filtered Drains* At the low point in vertical sections to prevent accumulation of condensation.

BUS MAINTENANCE

At periodic intervals buses should be inspected and maintained.

- Examine bolted bus joints for signs of heating or looseness. Check bolts for tightness per the vendor's recommendations.

- Examine bus insulators and insulation. Insulators and insulation should be cleaned. Do not use chemical solvents on insulation, because they may chemically react with the insulation.

- Bus coolers will require routine maintenance on moving parts:
  - Maintain motor (Volume 6)
  - Clean or replace air filters
  - Replace fan belts

Bus conductors will be copper or aluminum and plated with silver or tin at bolted joints. Note that silver is never plated directly onto aluminum because of galvanic problems. The plating procedure on aluminum has several intervening steps ending with copper, upon which the silver is plated. If the process is imperfect or the plating is scratched, galvanic action between the aluminum and silver will result in blistering and failure of the plating. Silver plating on aluminum should be kept covered with inert grease to eliminate this problem.

Tin plating on aluminum has been used successfully for 20 years and is recommended. Joint resistance will be slightly higher than with silver plating but is easily accommodated in the design.

7.11 ENVIRONMENTAL CONSIDERATIONS

Usual service conditions are defined as:

- Where the ambient temperature is not above 40°C or below −30°C
- Where the altitude is not above 3300 ft (1000 m)

Any conditions outside the "usual" service conditions are considered special and will require attention.

ABNORMAL TEMPERATURES

Abnormally low temperatures may result in circuit breaker malfunction due to congealed lubricants or increased friction due to parts shrinkage. Abnormally high temperatures may result in failure to interrupt rated short-circuit currents. In either case, the manufacturer should be consulted. Low temperatures may be remedied by special lubricants and parts selection. High temperatures may also require special lubricants and probably derating.

HIGH ALTITUDE

For applications at altitudes higher than 3300 ft (1000 m), the basic impulse level and rated maximum voltage must be reduced due to lower dielectric strength of the air. Also, the rated continuous current must be reduced due to lower convection loss through the air. Refer to ANSI/IEEE Standard C37.04-1979 (*4*) and ANSI Standard C37.010-1979/ IEEE Standard 320-1979 (*13*) for guidance.

HOSTILE ENVIRONMENT

In general, there are no remedies for exposure to abrasive dust, explosive dust or gas, steam, salt spray, excessive moisture, flooding, dripping, coal dust, or metal dust. These conditions must be avoided. Switchgear must have a clean, dry environment. If it must be placed in a hostile environment, a suitable enclosure must be provided to alleviate the unacceptable conditions. In some cases, positive pressure ventilation systems can be used. It must be emphasized that equipment failures are rarely due to a product deficiency; they are usually due to coal dust, cement dust, water leaking through the roof, unexpected flooding, and other environmental intrusions and often aggravated by little or no maintenance.

EXPOSURE TO ABNORMAL VIBRATION OR TILTING

Electrical equipment (switchgear) is designed to function in a normal industrial environment, one that is reasonably level and not subject to substantive vibration. Abnormal vibration and tilting may result in parts loosening and/or equipment malfunction. The manufacturer is the only sure guide, and the best remedy is avoidance. Note that some (usually smaller) devices are more resistant to the effects of vibration and tilting. Vibration isolation mounting may be available from the manufacturer.

EXPOSURE TO ATMOSPHERIC SULFUROUS GASES

Copper and silver are among the metals particularly sensitive to atmospheric corrosion, a property that limits their use in certain electrical applications. Corrosive films are responsible for the light green color that copper acquires after prolonged outdoor exposure.

For corrosion of copper or silver by sulfurous gases, the surface must be wet but does not require condensation. Hygroscopic salts on the metal surface, deposited or formed by corrosion, will absorb water from the atmosphere. Absorption occurs above a certain relative humidity, called the critical relative humidity, the value of which depends on the metal and surface contaminants. The critical relative humidity is probably between 50 and 70% (35).

Sulfates are known to form from various sulfurous corrodants:

Hydrogen sulfide	H_2S
Carbonyl sulfide	OCS
Sulphur dioxide	SO_2
Carbon disulfide	CS_2
Methyl mercaptan	CH_3SH
Dimethyl sulfide	CH_3SCH_3

(Free sulfur is not known to exist in the atmosphere.)

Although the corrodants are recognized, the corrosion mechanism has never been satisfactorily explained.

Exposure to sulfurous gases presents a serious threat to electrical equipment. These gases attack silver and copper and may grow "whiskers" on electrical contacts. Extended exposure to sulfurous gases may render electrical equipment unreliable and may be the direct cause of failure. Resistance to sulfurous gases must be specified when equipment is purchased and may require special contact material, special plating, and derating.

7.12   INSTALLATION REQUIREMENTS

Installation requirements are fundamental and must be considered when station layout is made and equipment selected. Considerations overlooked at the conceptual stage are rectified in the construction stage with great difficulty and generally result in delays in construction. Installation requirements that do not relate to construction such as lie-down space and equipment removal space present a burden and hazard to operating personnel throughout the life of the station. In summary, attention to installation requirements at the inception of a project is rewarded by minimum construction rework costs and safe station operation with minimum downtime.

When equipment is first installed, it should be checked for cleanliness, proper assembly, and function before being energized. The steps listed under "Recommended Scheduled Maintenance" in Section 7.13 may be followed, except there will be no evidence of abnormal wear or heating on new equipment.

INSTALLING VENTILATED DRY-TYPE TRANSFORMERS

Ventilated dry-type transformers must be acceptably dry before energizing, or the transformer may fail upon being energized. If an in-service transformer has been deenergized and allowed to cool to ambient temperature under humid conditions, lack of dryness may lead to failure. Further, if a transformer is known to be wet or subject to damp conditions, it should be dried irrespective of insulation resistance values.

Minimum insulation resistance values specified by the manufacturer should be met before energizing. If the manufacturer's recommended values are not available, the values in Table 7-3 (*36*) may be used.

Normally, dry transformers will have readings 5 to 10 times the above minimums.

Transformers may be dried before installation or after an extended shutdown by the following methods:

- Internal heat
- External heat
- External and internal heat

Refer to the vendor or ANSI/IEEE C57.94-1982 (*36*) for detailed drying recommendations.

Table 7.3 Minimum Values for Insulation Resistance

Winding kV Class	Insulation Resistance (MΩ)
1.2	600
2.5	1000
5.0	1500
8.7	2000
15.0	3000

ACCESSIBILITY AND PROVISION FOR REMOVAL

Adequate space must be provided for accessibility and normal operation of the equipment. As a minimum, the vendor's recommendations must be followed. This includes sufficient space to withdraw circuit breakers and other components and to provide sufficient working space for operation and maintenance. Note that clearances may be needed for other than purely mechanical reasons. Clearances may be required at the ends and top of equipment to ensure sufficient heat loss. Access to the rear is mandatory for all electrical equipment except motor control centers. Motor control centers are designed to have all components, including the bus, accessible from the front, permitting their mounting against a wall. Although mounting against a wall is permissible, rear access to motor control centers will reduce maintenance time and should be provided when possible.

7.13 MAINTENANCE REQUIREMENTS

An established regular maintenance schedule is required to maintain reliability. Plant operating and environmental conditions dictate the frequency of maintenance required; however, at the minimum, an 18-month maintenance is recommended. For specific information on maintenance of devices such as circuit breakers, relays, and other equipment, separate instruction books for each device are generally available. Under normal conditions, protective relays are not generally called on to function; thus, it is imperative to check functional operation of these devices regularly.

RECOMMENDED SCHEDULED MAINTENANCE

Switchgear should be given the following maintenance at regular intervals.

1. Thoroughly clean the equipment to remove dust and other accumulations. Wipe buses and supports. Inspect connections for evidence of overheating or insulation damage.

2. Insulation resistance and high-potential tests are not required and are not easily done on installed equipment. They may be done if there is reason to believe that dielectric integrity may be impaired, perhaps because of contamination, smoke, water damage, or other environmental intrusion.

   To obtain insulation resistance, measure resistance to ground between phases of the bus with with a 1000- or 2500-V Megger. Definite minimum resistance values cannot be given, but one rule is 1 MΩ for each 1000 V of operating voltage, with a minimum value of 1 MΩ. Note that insulation resistance will be halved for an 8° to 15°C temperature increase.

   High-voltage tests are pass-fail tests. The equipment withstands the voltage or fails. The advantage of high-voltage testing values as noted in Table 7-4 is that damage from a high-voltage test failure will be trivial compared with dielectric failure when in service. The field test voltage should not exceed 75% of the factory test voltage (*3*).

   Voltage transformers, control power transformers, lightning arrestors, and surge suppressors must be disconnected during high-voltage testing.

   Dc high-voltage testing on equipment above the 13.8-kV class should be done only with the vendor's approval. When testing with dc, voltage gradients will be determined solely by leakage resistance rather than distributed capacitance, and conceivably, good equipment may be damaged by the test.

Table 7.4 *Equipment High-Potential Test Voltages*

Nominal Voltage Class (kV)	Factory Test Voltage (kV)	Field Test Voltage (kV)	Field DC Test Voltage (kV)
0.6	2.2	1.65	2.3
4.16	19.0	14.25	20.25
7.2	26.0	19.5	27.5
13.8	36.0	27.0	37.5
14.4	50.0	37.5	52.5
23.0	60.0	45.0	
34.5	80.0	60.0	

3. Clean and lubricate the racking mechanism.

4. Check primary disconnect device contacts for abnormal wear or overheating. Discoloration of silvered surfaces is not harmful unless a chemically active atmosphere has generated sulfides on the surface.

Sandpaper, steel wool, or other abrasive cleaners should never be used on silver-plated parts. If necessary, silver polish may be used.

Before replacing the breaker, apply a thin coat of contact lubricant to primary disconnect contacts/studs.

5. Measure resistance of the circuit breaker contacts by making millivolt-drop tests or using a microohmmeter. Millivolt-drop tests are made by passing a substantial current (100 A is suggested) and measuring millivolt drop by placing voltmeter probes on the studs or conductors. Contact resistance may be calculated by using Ohm's law:

$$R = E/I \qquad \text{(Eq. 7-10)}$$

Where:

R = contact resistance

E = millivolt drop across contacts

I = circulated current

Note that a substantial current is used because nonlinearities may appear at low currents, giving resistance values that are invalid for higher-rated currents. Use vendor information for acceptability of contact resistance measurements.

6. Verify that anchor bolts and structural bolts are tight. Check tightness and continuity of all control connections and wiring.

7. If equipped with heaters, verify that all heaters are energized and operating.

8. Inspect and maintain air filters.

9. Inspect bolted electric bus joints for signs of overheating—discoloration and oxidation—and test for bolt tightness.

- *Bolts With Belleville Spring Washers* There are two schools of thought, and both are acceptable.
  - Tighten until the Belleville washer is flat. If the bolt is stretched beyond its elastic limit, the Belleville washer will take up the slack.
  - Tighten until the Belleville washer is flat and back off a vendor-specified amount. The Belleville washer will accommodate thermal expansion and contraction.

- *Bolts With Lockwashers (not lubricated)* Tighten to the manufacturer's specified torque, or the following (*37*), if none are given.

Bolt Diameter (silicon-bronze or steel)	*Torque (ft•lb)*
3/8	20
1/2	40
5/8	55

MAINTENANCE PROBLEMS UNIQUE TO EACH TYPE OF CIRCUIT BREAKER

There is great similarity among operating mechanisms for all circuit breakers; all use a four-bar mechanism to provide electrical and mechanical trip-free operation. However, there are maintenance problems and hazards unique to each type of circuit breaker. The vendor's instruction manual is the primary guide for maintenance of the circuit breaker. It will specify latch and roll clearances, recommended lubricants, contact pressure, and other mechanical adjustments.

Operating mechanism problems and approaches to solutions follow:

- Circuit breaker will not close, goes trip-free upon closing

  Check four-bar linkage
  Latch to roll clearance insufficient
  Latches not resetting
  Latch bite too small
  Latch worn

■ Circuit breaker will not close (solenoid operated)	Auxiliary switch b stage maladjusted Blown fuse in closing circuit Bad contacts in contactor Low voltage
(spring operated)	Spring-release coil is damaged Spring-release armature maladjusted
■ Circuit breaker is unstable, trips spontaneously	Latch bite too small Latch worn
■ Mechanism will not charge (motor-spring operated)	
□ Spring charging motor will not run	Defective motor Worn brushes Blown fuse Motor disconnect switch not reset (if furnished)
□ Spring charging motor runs, will not charge closing spring	Sheared key on cam Spring-release latch not holding—no roll clearance, latch not resetting, latch worn
■ Circuit breaker will not trip	Blown fuse in trip circuit Trip coil damaged Trip armature maladjusted Auxiliary switch a stage maladjusted Low voltage

Air-Magnetic Circuit Breakers The major components of air-magnetic circuit breakers that require the most maintenance include the arcing contacts, which are considered expendable components, the main current-carrying contacts, and the arc chutes. Care should be exercised when maintaining the arc chutes in older equipment that may contain asbestos. Loose asbestos, which may be inhaled, is a serious health hazard. When working with loose asbestos particles, vacuum to remove loose particles, maintain adequate ventilation, and use approved breathing apparatus. Material with embedded asbestos is not considered a health hazard unless it is abraded or machined, releasing loose asbestos.

Air-magnetic circuit breaker problems and approaches to solutions follow:

■ High resistance through contacts	Clean, adjust, replace contacts; adjust contact pressure
■ Slow circuit breaker operation, erratic operation	Interference in moving parts

Oil Circuit Breakers Oil circuit breakers may require maintenance in three areas: main and arcing contacts, interrupting devices, and condition of the oil.

■ Examine contacts for excessive erosion and wear. Arc tracks and small pits on the arcing contacts are acceptable. Contacts with heavy erosion or cracks should be replaced. Current-carrying contacts excessively scored or worn should be replaced. Contact pressure springs may anneal, causing inadequate pressure and resulting in contact overheating and burning.

■ Interrupting devices are commonly made with fiber or plastic components. These components erode during interruption and should be replaced when erosion is noticeable. Excessive contact erosion may be caused by severely eroded interrupting devices.

■ Oil is carbonized during operation of the circuit breaker. Large particles will settle to the bottom of the tank, and small particles will remain in suspension. There are many tests used to evaluate the quality of insulating oil (38), but the best criterion of oil quality for circuit breaker applications is dielectric strength. Oil should be drawn from the bottom of the tank, after running off oil containing any sediment or free water that may be present. The oil test cup has disk electrodes 1.0 in. (25 mm) in diameter with square corners, spaced 0.100 in. (2.54 mm). It is filled with oil to a depth of at least 0.80 in. (20 mm) above the disks. Voltage is applied (60 cycle), increasing at a rate of 3 kV ± 20% (rms) per second until continuous breakdown is achieved. Occasional momentary discharges that do not result in a permanent arc may occur and should be disregarded (39). A minimum breakdown voltage of 25-kV rms is acceptable for oil circuit breakers.

Note that it is essential that good hygienic practice be followed by those working with insulating oil. Liquid contact is irritating to the eyes and, when repeated or prolonged, to the skin. Wash exposed skin areas with soap and water several times during the working day. Oil-soaked clothing should not be worn. Work clothes should be laundered at least once a week.

- No continuity through contacts
  Broken lift rod, check shock absorber
  Deteriorated contacts

- Excessive oil throw upon operation
  Low opening velocity
  Circuit breaker may be overloaded
  Interrupting devices badly eroded

Vacuum Circuit Breakers Vacuum circuit breakers require significantly less maintenance than air-magnetic or oil circuit breakers. The vacuum interrupter is a sealed unit, and obviously no work can be done on the contact structure.

Indeed, in most cases it cannot even be seen. Contact erosion may be measured by mechanical adjustment, and a high-potential (hi-pot) test is recommended to verify vacuum integrity. Contact resistance may be measured by a millivolt-drop test or with a microohmmeter and should be within the manufacturer's acceptable range.

When applying abnormally high voltage across a pair of contacts in a vacuum, X rays may be generated. Radiation may increase with an increase in voltage, and/or decrease in contact spacing. X radiation produced during hi-pot testing at recommended voltages and contact spacing is extremely low and well below the maximum permitted by standards. However, as a precautionary measure, it is recommended that personnel stay at least 1 m away from and in front of the circuit breaker during high-pot testing.

Air-Blast Circuit Breakers Air-blast circuit breakers will principally require maintenance in the contacts, compressor-air control valves, and arc chutes.

- Contacts are treated in the same way as are oil circuit breakers.

- The compressor will run periodically whether the circuit breaker is operated or not and will require maintenance. Special attention must be given to the air-drying device to ensure clean, dry air.

- Control valves may fail to operate properly due to worn seals. A preventive maintenance/replacement schedule is recommended to preclude failure.

- Arc chutes will show erosion and should be replaced when it becomes significant. Excessive contact erosion may be caused by severely eroded arc chutes.

SF₆ Circuit Breakers The amount of maintenance required for SF_6 circuit breakers is a function of the circuit breaker size and design. SF_6 equipment rated for 72 kV and above has become well known. At these levels, it is not unusual to be concerned about large volumes of gas, leaks, gas contamination, and complex apparatus. At medium-voltage levels, design and materials have overcome almost all maintenance requirements associated with high-voltage designs. Continuous cast epoxy envelopes and special liquid gas seals have created permanently sealed interrupters that are precharged at the factory. The gas need not be checked unless the operational policy dictates. Serviceability can be checked by observation of contact wear by external means. Contact wear and mechanism lubrication might be considered every two or three years depending upon the number of operations. Typical load-break operations range from 5000 to 10,000 uses without service, depending upon break type.

SF_6 is an excellent interrupting and insulating medium. There are, however, some precautions in the use of the SF_6 gas. In the medium-voltage levels, the volume of gas per interrupter is very small. The volume of gas of a 38-kV, 32-kA interrupter would expand to 0.5 ft³ at atmospheric pressures. Considering the density is five times that of air, it would be extremely difficult to obtain concentrations of gas sufficiently high under normal conditions to cause any concern.

Although SF_6 is highly stable, high-temperature decomposition and recombination lead to formation of lower fluorides of sulfur, metal sulfurs, and metal fluorides, most of which are toxic.

$$SF_6 \xrightarrow{\text{electric arc, etc.}} SF_6 + SF_4 + SF_2 + S_2F_2 + S_2F_{10} + \cdots \quad \textbf{(Eq. 7-11)}$$

In the presence of moisture, oxyfluorides, hydrogen fluoride (HF), thionylfluoride (SOF_2), and sulfur dioxide (SO_2) are produced.

$$SF_4 \xrightarrow{H_2O} SOF_2 + 2HF \qquad \textbf{(Eq. 7-12)}$$

$$SOF_2 \xrightarrow{H_2O} SO_2 + 2HF \qquad \textbf{(Eq. 7-13)}$$

Most of the decomposition products are highly reactive, highly toxic, and many are odorless. Fortunately, most are unstable in the presence of moisture or metal from the enclosure and will not be found except perhaps in event of a burn-through or immediate opening of the enclosure after arcing. The major enduring gaseous decomposition products are as follows in order of expected volume.

Thionylfluoride (SOF_2) is the major arcing product. It irritates the eyes, throat, and lungs. It is detectable at 1 to 5 ppm by its characteristic rotten-egg smell. The 60-min lethal concentration is near 100 ppm.

Carbon tetrafluoride (CF_4) gas is odorless but relatively nontoxic. It is also known as Freon 14. CF_4 may also be found in new, unused SF_6.

Sulfur dioxide may be found in trace amounts. It is not stable in the presence of moisture; it converts to sulfurous acid (H_2SO_3). Sulfur dioxide has an acrid smell detectable at 0.3 to 1 ppm. The gas damages the lungs and is lethal at 400 to 500 ppm.

Hydrogen fluoride is extremely corrosive and is classified as an irritant gas. Fortunately it is easily recognized by its pungent smell at concentrations of 2 to 3 ppm.

In the event of a fault causing a large toxic gas spill, employees should immediately vacate the premises and ventilate the area.

When handling newly delivered SF_6, an electric or gas heater should not be employed because at temperatures encountered in electric and gas heaters, SF_6 can also form toxic by-products.

When disassembling a tank, powdery products may be found, presumably metal sulfides, fluorides, and metal sulfates. They may be hazardous to maintenance personnel because their toxicity has not been determined. The powders must not be touched or inhaled and should be removed by vacuum cleaner. (Refer to manufacturer's instructions.) If it is necessary to enter a circuit breaker chamber, protective clothing and breathing apparatus are appropriate. (One would not enter a medium-voltage interrupter as it is too small.)

It is worth noting that the leakage rate in normal operation, perhaps 1% per year, presents a negligible risk of asphyxiation. Even in a gastight room, after one year's operation the concentration of gas would be within acceptable limits.

For further discussion, refer to EPRI EL-1646, *Study of Arc By-Products in Gas-insulated Equipment (40)*.

REFERENCES

1. S. F. Farog and R. G. Bartheld. "Guidelines for the Application of Vacuum Contactors." In *IEEE Transactions on Industry Applications*, vol. IA-22, no. 1. New York: Institute of Electrical and Electronics Engineers, January/February 1986, pp. 102–8.

2. *Switchgear Assemblies Including Metal-enclosed Bus.* New York: American National Standards Institute, 1974. ANSI Std. C37.20-1969/IEEE Std. 27-1974.

3. *Preferred Ratings and Related Required Capabilities for AC High-Voltage Circuit Breakers Rated on a Symmetrical-Current Basis.* New York: American National Standards Institute, 1979. ANSI Std. C37.06-1979.

4. *Rating Structure for AC High-Voltage Circuit Breakers Rated on a Symmetrical Current Basis.* New York: American National Standards Institute, 1979. ANSI/IEEE Std. C37.04-1979.

5. *Definitions and Rating Structure for AC High-Voltage Circuit Breakers Rated on a Total Current Basis.* New York: American National Standards Institute, 1953. ANSI Std. C37.4-1953.

6. *Methods for Determining the RMS Value of a Sinusoidal Current Wave and Normal Frequency Recovery Voltage, and for Simplified Calculations of Fault Currents.* New York: American National Standards Institute, 1953. ANSI Std. C37.5-1953.

7. *Schedules of Preferred Ratings for Power Circuit Breakers.* New York: American National Standards Institute, 1953. ANSI Std. C37.6-1953.

8. *Interrupting Rating Factors for Reclosing Services.* New York: American National Standards Institute, 1952. ANSI Std. C37.7-1952.

9. *Rated Control Voltages and Their Ranges.* New York: American National Standards Institute, 1952. ANSI Std. C37.8-1952.

10. *Test Code for Power Circuit Breakers.* New York: American National Standards Institute, 1953. ANSI Std. C37.9-1953.

11. *Guide to Specifications for Alternating Current Power Circuit Breakers.* New York: American National Standards Institute, 1981. ANSI Std. C37.12-1981.

12. *Test Procedures for AC High-Voltage Circuit Breakers Rated on a Symmetrical Current Basis.* New York: American National Standards Institute, 1979. ANSI/IEEE Std. C37.09-1979.

13. *Application Guide for AC High-Voltage Circuit Breakers Rated on a Symmetrical Current Basis.* New York: American National Standards Institute, 1979. ANSI Std. C37.010-1979/IEEE Std. 320-1979.

14. *Application Guide for Transient Recovery Voltages for AC High-Voltage Circuit Breakers Rated on a Symmetrical Current Basis.* New York: American National Standards Institute, 1979. ANSI/IEEE Std. C37.011-1979.

15. *Application Guide for Capacitance Current Switching of AC High-Voltage Circuit Breakers Rated on a Symmetrical Current Basis.* New York: American National Standards Institute, 1979. ANSI/IEEE Std. C37.012-1979.

16. *IEEE Standard for Emergency Load Current-carrying Capability.* New York: American National Standards Institute, 1985. ANSI/IEEE Std. C37.010b-1985 (supplement to ANSI/IEEE C37.010-1979).

17. W. G. Heinmiller, R. W. Katterhenry, and S. R. Lambert. "Transient Recovery Voltage Failures of Two 15-kV Indoor Oilless Circuit Breakers." In *IEEE Transactions on Power Apparatus and Systems*, vol. PAS-102, no. 8. New York: Institute of Electrical and Electronics Engineers, August 1983, pp. 2578–84.

18. N. Irving Sax. *Dangerous Properties of Industrial Materials.* New York: Van Nostrand Reinhold Co., 1984.

19. *Maintenance and Handling of Perchloroethylene-filled Electrical Equipment.* Palo Alto, Calif.: Electric Power Research Institute, January 1986. EL-4407.

20. "Freon 113 Material Safety Data Sheet." Wilmington, Del.: E. I. du Pont de Nemours & Co., October 1985. E-77815-1, rev. 10/85.

21. "Freon Fluorocarbons: Properties and Applications." Wilmington, Del.: E. I. du Pont de Nemours & Co. G-1, E-03528-1, rev. 3/85.

22. *Preferred Ratings, Related Requirements, and Application Recommendations for Low-Voltage Power Circuit Protectors.* New York: American National Standards Institute, 1980. ANSI Std. C37.16-1980.

23. *Low-Voltage AC Power Circuit Breakers Used in Enclosures.* New York: American National Standards Institute, 1981. ANSI Std. C37.13-1981.

24. *Recommended Practice for Electric Power Distribution Plants.* New York: Institute of Electrical and Electronics Engineers, 1976. IEEE Std. 141-1976.

25. *Recommended Practice for Electric Power Systems in Commercial Buildings.* New York: Institute of Electrical and Electronics Engineers. ANSI/IEEE Std. 241-1983.

26. *Recommended Practice for Protection and Coordination of Industrial and Commercial Power Systems.* New York: Institute of Electrical and Electronics Engineers, 1975. IEEE Std. 242-1975.

27. *General Standards for Industrial Control and Systems.* Washington, D.C.: National Electrical Manufacturers Association, 1983. NEMA Std. ICS 1-1983.

28. *Industrial Control Devices, Controllers, and Assemblies.* Washington, D.C.: National Electrical Manufacturers Association, 1983. NEMA Std. ICS 2-1983.

29. *Terminal Blocks for Industrial Control Equipment and Systems.* Washington, D.C.: National Electrical Manufacturers Association, 1983. NEMA Std. ICS 4-1983.

30. *Enclosures for Industrial Controls and Systems.* Washington, D.C.: National Electrical Manufacturers Association, 1983. NEMA Std. ICS 6-1983.

31. *Panel Boards.* Washington, D.C.: National Electrical Manufacturers Association, 1984. NEMA Std. PB 1-1984.

32. *Molded-Case Circuit Breakers.* Washington, D.C.: National Electrical Manufacturers Association, 1975. NEMA Std. AB 1-1975.

33. *Procedures for Verifying the Performance of Molded-Case Circuit Breakers.* Washington, D.C.: National Electrical Manufacturers Association, 1976. NEMA Std. AB 2-1976.

34. *Guide for Evaluating the Effects of Solar Radiation on Outdoor Metal-Clad Switchgear.* New York: American National Standards Institute, 1971. ANSI Std. C37.24-1971.

35. *Corrosion Source Book.* Houston, Texas: National Association of Corrosion Engineers, 1984.

36. *Recommended Practice for Installation, Application, Operation, and Maintenance of Dry-Type General Purpose Distribution and Power Transformers.* New York: American National Standards Institute, 1982. ANSI/IEEE Std. C57.94-1982.

37. *Electric Power Connections for Substations.* Washington, D.C.: National Electrical Manufacturers Association, 1981. NEMA Std. CC 1-1981.

38. *Mineral Insulating Oil Used in Electrical Apparatus.* Philadelphia, Pa.: American Society of Testing Materials, 1982. ASTM D-3487-82.

39. *Standard Test Method for Dielectric Breakdown Voltage of Insulation Liquids Using Disk Electrodes.* Philadelphia, Pa.: American Society of Testing Materials, 1984. ASTM D-877-84.

40. *Arc By-Products in Gas-insulated Equipment.* Palo Alto, Calif.: Electric Power Research Institute, December 1980. EL-1646.

BIBLIOGRAPHY

"Bibliography of Switchgear Literature." In *IEEE Transactions on Power Apparatus and Systems*, vol. PAS-104, no. 12. New York: Institute of Electrical and Electronics Engineers, December 1985, pp. 3643–56.

Burkhardt, P., E. Vadasgi, and M. Seidel. "DC Generator Breakers for Extremely High Service and Short-Circuit Currents." *Brown-Boveri Review*, vol. 64, no. 4, April 4, 1975, pp. 131–38.

Conangla, Amado, and Harris F. White. "Isolated-Phase Bus Enclosure Loss Factors." In *IEEE Transactions on Power Apparatus and Systems*, vol. PAS-87, no. 7. New York: Institute of Electrical and Electronics Engineers, July 1968, pp. 1622–28.

Controlled Impedance Short-Circuit Limiter. Palo Alto, Calif.: Electric Power Research Institute, September 1977. EL-537.

Controlled Impedance Short-Circuit Limiter. Palo Alto, Calif.: Electric Power Research Institute, August 1978. EL-857.

Criteria for Class 1E Power Systems for Nuclear Power Generating Stations. New York: Institute of Electrical and Electronics Engineers, 1980. IEEE Std. 308-1980.

Development of a Circuit Breaker for Large Generators. Palo Alto, Calif.: Electric Power Research Institute, January 1982. EL-2195.

Development of a Current Limiter Using Vacuum Arc Commutation, Phase 1: A Feasibility Study for Using Arc Instability in Vacuum for Current Limitation. Palo Alto, Calif.: Electric Power Research Institute, March 1977. EL-393.

Development of Current-limiting Conductor. Palo Alto, Calif.: Electric Power Research Institute, February 1977. EL-286.

Development of Distribution and Subtransmission SF$_6$ Circuit Breaker and Hybrid Transmission Interruptor. Palo Alto, Calif.: Electric Power Research Institute, June 1978. EL-810.

Durso, R. G. "Restoring Flood-damaged Electrical Equipment." *Plant Engineering*, vol. 34, no. 13, June 26, 1980, pp. 87–90.

Dwight, H. B. "Some Proximity Effect Formulas for Bus Enclosures." In *IEEE Transactions on Power Apparatus and Systems*, vol. PAS-83. New York: American Institute of Electrical and Electronics Engineers, December 1964, pp. 1167–72.

Elgar, Everett C., Robert H. Rehder, and Nathan Swerdlow. "Measured Losses in Isolated-Phase Bus and Comparison With Calculated Values." In *AIEE Transactions on Power Apparatus and Systems*, vol. PAS-87. New York: American Institute of Electrical Engineers (now Institute of Electrical and Electronics Engineers), August 1968, pp. 1724–30.

Engmann, G. R., and A. D. McCown. "Expected Switching Life for Safety-related Metal Clad Switchgear Applied in a Boiling Water Reactor Generating Unit." In *IEEE Transactions on Power Apparatus and Systems*, vol. PAS-100, no. 5. New York: Institute of Electrical and Electronics Engineers, May 1981, pp. 2459–63.

Fault Analysis in Gas-insulated Equipment. Palo Alto, Calif.: Electric Power Research Institute, February 1980. EL-2248.

Fault Detection Sensors for Gas-insulated Equipment. Palo Alto, Calif.: Electric Power Research Institute, February 1982. EL-2249.

Fundamental Investigation of Arc Interruption in Gas Flows. Palo Alto, Calif.: Electric Power Research Institute, January 1977. EL-284.

Guide for Calculating Losses in Isolated-Phase Bus. New York: American National Standards Institute, 1969. ANSI/IEEE Std. 37.23-1969.

"High-Voltage Circuit Breaker Standards in the U.S.A.—Past, Present, and Future." In *IEEE Transactions on Power Apparatus and Systems*, vol. PAS-98. New York: Institute of Electrical and Electronics Engineers, January–June 1974, pp. 590–600.

IEEE Guide for Temperature Correlation in the Connection of Insulated Wire and Cables to Electronic Equipment. New York: Institute of Electrical and Electronics Engineers, 1955. IEEE Std. 55-1593.

Investigation of Feasibility of Vacuum Arc Fault-Current Limiting Device. Palo Alto, Calif.: Electric Power Research Institute, December 1977. EL-538.

Janssen, F. J. G. *Measurements at the Sub-ppm Level of Sulfur-Fluoride Compounds Resulting From the Decomposition of SF$_6$ by Arc Discharge.* KEMA Scientific and Technical Report, vol. 2, no. 2. Arnhem, The Netherlands: N. V. KEMA, 1984, pp. 9–18.

Kennedy, G. P. "Application of Motor Control Centers to Systems Having High Available Fault Currents." In *IEEE Transactions on Industry Applications*, vol. 1A-9, no. 6. New York: Institute of Electrical and Electronics Engineers, November/December 1973, pp. 666–71.

Kubica, P., and D. J. Love. "Generator Breaker Provides Advantages Over Unit Connection." *Power Engineering*, vol. 86, no. 5, May 1982, pp. 54–57.

Low-Voltage DC Power Circuit Breakers and Anode Circuit Breakers. New York: American National Standards Institute, 1969. ANSI Std. C37.14-1969.

Modeling of Arc Discharges in Power Circuit Breakers. Palo Alto, Calif.: Electric Power Research Institute, November 1977. EL-482.

Niemoller, A. B. "Isolated-Phase Bus Enclosure Currents." In *IEEE Transactions on Power Apparatus and Systems,* vol. PAS-87. New York: American Institute of Electrical and Electronics Engineers, August 1968, pp. 1714–18.

Preferred Power Supply for Nuclear Power Generating Stations. New York: Institute of Electrical and Electronics Engineers, 1983. IEEE Std. 765-1983.

Safety Requirements for X-Radiation Limits for AC High-Voltage Power Vacuum Interruptors Used in Power Switchgear. New York: American National Standards Institute, 1972.

Salzer, E., Sr. *Fundamentals of AC Circuit Interruption.* Milwaukee, Wisc.: Allis-Chalmers Manufacturing Co., 1950. Publication no. 71R7396.

Schaumann, R., and I. Poole. "The H System—A New Generation of SF$_6$ Medium Voltage Switchgear." *Brown-Boveri Review,* vol. 64, no. 11, November 1977, pp. 644–49.

Standard for Motor Control Centers. Northbrook, Ill.: Underwriters' Laboratory, 1980. UL-845-1980.

Standard for Unit Substations. Northbrook, Ill.: Underwriters' Laboratory, 1983. UL-1062-1983.

Swerdlow, Nathan, and M. A. Buchta. "Practical Solutions of Inductive Heating Problems Resulting From High Current Buses." In *AIEE Transactions,* vol. 78, part IIIB. New York: American Institute of Electrical Engineers, 1959, pp. 1736–46.

Symposium Proceedings: New Concepts in Fault Current Limiters and Power Circuit Breakers. Palo Alto, Calif.: Electric Power Research Institute, April 1977. EL-276-SR.

Theoret, D. A., and R. Gilbert. "Occupational Hazards and Other Problems Related to the Use of Sulfur Hexafluoride in Metal-Clad Substations." *Canadian Electrical Engineering Journal,* vol. 1, no. 4, 1976, pp. 24–28.

Wilson, J. C., and H. S. Robinson. "Application of Motor Control Centers With Molded-Case Circuit Breakers in Systems with High-Fault Capability." In *IEEE Transactions on Industrial Applications,* vol. 1A-10, no. 1. New York: Institute of Electrical and Electronics Engineers, January/February 1974, pp. 66–80.

Wilson, W. R., and L. L. Mankoff. "Short-Circuit Forces in Isolated-Phase Bus." In *AIEE Transactions,* vol. 73, pt. IIIA. New York: American Institute of Electrical Engineers, April 1954, pp. 382–96.

INDEX

VOLUME **7**

AUXILIARY ELECTRICAL EQUIPMENT

ELECTRIC POWER RESEARCH INSTITUTE
3412 Hillview Avenue
Palo Alto, CA 94304

To help EPRI improve future editions of this volume, your comments on the following would be greatly appreciated:

1. Please list the topics or areas that you felt were well covered.

2. What technical and/or editorial improvements would you like to see?

3. Please note any technical and/or editorial mistakes you discovered in this volume.

Please fold this questionnaire and mail to EPRI. No postage is necessary.

BUSINESS REPLY MAIL
FIRST CLASS   PERMIT NO. 586   PALO ALTO, CA 94303

POSTAGE WILL BE PAID BY ADDRESSEE

ELECTRIC POWER RESEARCH INSTITUTE
Attn: D. K. Sharma
P.O. Box 10412
Palo Alto, CA 94303

NO POSTAGE
NECESSARY
IF MAILED
IN THE
UNITED STATES